DEVELOPiNG

LiTERHCiES

DEVELOPiNG DiGiTAL LiTERACiES

A Framework for Professional Learning

Dustin C. Summey

Foreword by Patrick Larkin

CORWIN
A SAGE Company

CORWIN
A SAGE Company

FOR INFORMATION:

Corwin

A SAGE Company

2455 Teller Road

Thousand Oaks, California 91320

(800) 233-9936

www.corwin.com

SAGE Publications Ltd.

1 Oliver's Yard

55 City Road

London, EC1Y 1SP

United Kingdom

SAGE Publications India Pvt. Ltd.

B 1/I 1 Mohan Cooperative Industrial Area

Mathura Road, New Delhi 110 044

India

SAGE Publications Asia-Pacific Pte. Ltd.

3 Church Street

#10-04 Samsung Hub

Singapore 049483

Acquisitions Editor: Arnis Burvikovs

Associate Editor: Desireé A. Bartlett

Editorial Assistant: Mayan White

Production Editor: Jane Haenel

Copy Editor: Beth Hammond

Typesetter: Hurix Systems Private Ltd.

Proofreader: Joyce Li

Indexer: Michael Ferreira

Cover Designer: Scott Van Atta

Marketing Manager: Stephanie Trkay

Permissions Editor: Jennifer Barron

Printed in the United States of America

A catalog record of this book is available from the Library of Congress.

978-1-4522-5552-1

This book is printed on acid-free paper.

13 14 15 16 17 10 9 8 7 6 5 4 3 2 1

Contents

Foreword

Sit back for a minute and think about the number of changes a teacher of 15 years has seen in his or her decade and a half in the classroom. It is very likely that this individual has transitioned from chalkboard, to whiteboard, to interactive whiteboard, to tablet, and is wondering what is coming next.

As a matter of fact, this question of *what's next* is probably on the minds of all educators regardless of their experience. We live in a day and age where yesterday's *new thing* can have a very short shelf life (i.e., Flip Cameras). While it is exciting to be teaching in a time where technologies are available that allow us to engage students in ways we never dreamed of, it can also be overwhelming. How can teachers stay up to speed when new devices, apps, and web-based resources are multiplying at a dizzying pace?

Adding to the complexity of this issue is the fact that most schools do not spend an ample amount of time providing focused professional development for the integration of new resources into the classroom. After spending large amounts of money to buy stuff, there seems to be little evidence that there was any thought given to support teachers (and students) in using the stuff.

Fortunately, there are examples of schools where the support of teachers in integrating technological resources has been done thoughtfully and in a manner that can be replicated. One person who has orchestrated the type of meaningful professional development necessary to take advantage of the infusion of technological resources in classrooms is Dustin Summey, the author of this book. Summey, an expert in instructional design, provides a concrete framework that can be utilized for district and school administrators as they work on visioning or by individual teachers as they look to enhance their ability to access and integrate technological resources in their classrooms.

In fact, the format described by Summey can be accomplished with little or no additional budgetary implications. The approach taken is one that builds internal capacity by letting teachers take the lead and share best practices. If schools are going to be able to move forward in the teaching of digital literacies to students, then they need to embrace a thoughtful professional development approach like this one that focuses on a school-wide understanding of these literacies by faculty and staff.

Our students need to be prepared for a world in which the acquisition of digital literacies is at a premium; therefore, we cannot leave it to chance that our teachers will grasp these skills on their own. Communication and collaboration have always been important skills for our students to master, but in the structure of many schools, they have not been modeled well. We are so fortunate to be living in a time where the development of digital tools makes communication and collaboration easier than it has ever been. A thoughtful reading of this book and the use of the reflective questions at the end of each chapter will assist school communities in filling this void.

Numerous reports say that our students will be applying for jobs that do not yet exist. In order to best prepare them for this, we need to change the way we do business in our schools. The examples provided throughout this book can help educators meet this challenge.

Patrick Larkin

2012 NASSP Digital Principal Award Winner

Assistant Superintendent for Learning

Burlington Public Schools, Massachusetts

Preface

*T*his is a book about professional development that supports teaching and learning with technology. It presents a highly adaptable framework for professional learning that enables teachers to infuse digital literacies into classroom instruction. Digital literacies are defined here as the essential skills for managing information and communication in the rapidly changing and increasingly digital world that is the 21st century.

Approaching technology through the lens of digital literacies facilitates the development of teachers and students as tech-savvy digital citizens with skills and competencies that can adapt to technology that is constantly evolving. When teachers and students learn to leverage information and communication technologies in order to *locate and filter, share and collaborate, organize and curate, create and generate, and reuse and repurpose,* they become fluent in digital literacies.

This paradigm shift in technology-infused teaching and learning can only happen when first modeled and then supported by high-quality professional development that is ongoing and embedded within the broader scope of professional growth activities. The approach described in this book capitalizes on personnel and resources that are already available internally. In fact, the program implementation that this book draws from was accomplished with a zero budget and no new hires. The use of teacher leaders and a train-the-trainer model means that not only responsibility but also ownership of the program is shared among the faculty. This leads to less burden on individuals and increased buy-in by participants.

This is not a one-shot, hit-or-miss approach. Readers are guided through the process of planning and implementing a digital literacies professional development emphasis and leveraging buy-in across the board. *This is one of those rare books that bridges the gap between knowing and doing.* Teachers become empowered to harness existing technologies and readily accessible digital resources in order to build upon their own teaching expertise and change the way students learn.

Rationale and Origin

This book is in many ways a result of my active and continued involvement in professional development leadership over many years and in diverse contexts. Those experiences have certainly afforded me a unique perspective. Technology-related professional development too often seems to fall short of equipping teachers to make full and appropriate use of the resources that schools spend huge amounts of money on. It is my desire through this book to encourage a more comprehensive, sustained approach to instructional technology integration at all levels.

The inspiration for this book came from an extensive professional development program I had the privilege of developing and facilitating as a faculty member serving in the role of a teacher leader. The challenges and successes of that initiative have informed many aspects of the professional development framework presented here.

My hope is that readers will find this book to be refreshingly practical. I have aimed to address many of the common problems that too often seem to be ignored. At the same time, I qualify my recommendations by acknowledging the reality that each context is unique and there is no single method that meets every possible need.

Intended Audiences and Suggested Uses

This book is intended to be read by teachers, principals, staff developers, curriculum directors, instructional technology coordinators, and other academic leaders at both the school and district levels. Advanced technological knowledge is *not* needed, although tech-savvy educators will definitely find the book to be relevant and challenging. Administrators and teacher leaders can use it during vision building and planning, and then as a guide to developing and implementing professional development—whether as a full-scale initiative or as a smaller piece of a broader effort. The concepts and ideas are certainly applicable at all grade levels and can be adapted to meet the needs of teachers and students in both upper and lower grades. This book is also designed to be used for a faculty book study. Questions located at the end of each chapter may be used to generate discussion and encourage practical application and timely results.

Format and Approach

The core of this book focuses on professional development, describing a modular framework that is both innovative and practical. Surrounding this is a carefully measured treatment of digital literacies and the information and communication technologies (i.e., technology tools) that go along with them. This intentional balance results in *an in-depth professional development resource complete with the technology-related supports to enable school-wide curriculum integration.*

Chapter 1, "New Literacies in a Digital World," sets the stage by establishing a scope and definition for digital literacies in order to frame the discussion into something that can be applied in diverse contexts.

Chapter 2, "Professional Development That (Really) Works," describes the traits that tend to characterize effective professional development and provides strategies for planning, marketing, implementation, and follow-up. It also takes a fresh look at both traditional and innovative models of professional learning. Common problems are addressed by providing practical solutions.

Chapter 3, "A Framework for Program Development and Implementation," is in many ways the heart of the book. This chapter presents a modular framework for developing and implementing professional development to support the integration of digital literacies into teaching and learning. Rather than adopting a singular model, it capitalizes on the best of several approaches, including among others, the professional learning community, peer mentoring, and personal learning networks. One of the unique aspects of the approach described is the degree to which the digital literacies are embedded throughout all aspects of the program.

Chapter 4, "Teacher Leaders and Support Structures," describes key roles within the context of the framework presented in the previous chapter and discusses administrative leadership while emphasizing the use of teacher leaders. It also suggests effective approaches for establishing both human and technological support systems.

Chapter 5, "Promoting Buy-In and Active Participation," gives focused attention to an often-overlooked aspect—marketing—that can be a game changer for powerful professional development. Anecdotes and cases are shared in order to illustrate these ideas in action in real situations.

Chapter 6, "Long-Term Planning: Ensuring a Lasting Impact," encourages long-term planning and foresight by providing methods and tools that can be used to ensure that digital literacies become well-embedded into the school-wide curriculum far beyond the conclusion of the professional development emphasis. A phased plan for training and support that looks at year one, two, three, and beyond can provide for a successful program that yields lasting results.

While technology skill acquisition is not the primary purpose here, it is a natural part of developing such digital literacies. Chapter 7, "The Tools of Technology," takes a look at the information and communication technologies that are widely considered to be new genres in digital literacies. Strategies and resources are provided for addressing each technology within the professional development program as a whole and ultimately integrating it into classroom instruction. *This final chapter also serves as a sort of technical reference, and readers may wish to refer to it periodically throughout the book when various technologies are mentioned in context.*

Open source tools referenced at various points are readily available on the Internet for enabling the technology integration that is needed within professional development and in classroom instruction.

Companion Website

The book's companion website (http://www.digitalliteracies.net) includes electronic versions of planning and implementation materials, sample instructional tools, and links to additional supporting resources such as tutorials, lesson ideas, and multimedia content that will further enable a successful professional development initiative and ultimately effective integration into classroom instruction.

Acknowledgments

Writing this book was in no way a solo endeavor. I owe my deepest appreciation to the numerous colleagues, friends, and family members who have made invaluable contributions toward the development of this book in the form of encouragement, creativity, and expertise.

I am grateful to Kevin Costley and Deborah Barber for the initial encouragement to write a book and to Deb Stollenwerk for believing in my idea. Patty Phelps, Vicki Parish, and Paige Rose were excellent sounding boards and lent their creative talent to the book-writing effort on many occasions. There are so many others who have played equally important roles in bringing this book to life.

It is a privilege to have the opportunity to be a teacher of teachers. Thousands of educators nationwide have graciously allowed me to learn alongside them while also empowering me to support their own professional growth. This book might not exist, were it not for the diverse opportunities I was afforded while on the faculty at Russellville High School in Russellville, Arkansas. I learned so much working with the teachers and administrators at Russellville, and the relationships that developed during that time continue to have a significant influence on me as an educator. I especially appreciate Wesley White and Margaret Robinson, who at that time were principal and assistant principal and who called upon me to develop the digital literacies emphasis that ultimately inspired this book.

Writing this book has been a professional learning experience in itself. I have had wonderful editorial support from Desirée Bartlett and Arnis Burvikovs, to whom I owe much appreciation for making the entire process such an enjoyable and fulfilling experience. Thank you!

Publisher's Acknowledgments

Corwin would like to thank the following individuals for taking the time to provide their editorial insight and guidance:

Barbara Cavanah, Technology Specialist
Monroe County School District
Marathon, FL

Beverly Ginther, Retired Staff Development Coordinator
Minnetonka Public Schools
Minnetonka, MN

Renee Peoples, Third Grade Teacher
West Elementary School
Bryson City, NC

Dr. Judith A. Rogers, K-5 Mathematics Specialist
Tucson Unified School District
Tucson, AZ

Kathy Tritz-Rhodes, Principal
Marcus-Meriden-Cleghorn Schools
Marcus, IA

Dr. Lee Ann Dubert Tysseling, Associate Professor of Literacy
Boise State University
Boise, ID

About the Author

 **Dustin C. Summey** is an instructional design specialist in the Instructional Development Center at the University of Central Arkansas in Conway, where he plans and implements faculty development for online course design and delivery and teaches courses in educational leadership and technology in the College of Education. He has taught multimedia, business, technology, fine arts, and music courses at the high school level in both traditional and online environments and continues to remain actively involved in K-12 teacher professional development. While teaching at Russellville High School (Arkansas), he provided extensive leadership in technology professional development and created and implemented a school-wide digital literacies initiative. He is active as a speaker, trainer, and consultant. His research interests include digital literacies, professional development, distance education, mobile learning, and music technology. Find him online at http://www.dustinsummey.com, and follow him on Twitter @dustinsummey.

1

New Literacies in a Digital World

Literacy and technology. These two words strike a chord within every educator. They evoke a myriad of emotions, ideas, and dispositions. As pillars of modern education, each stands to be an essential tenet of any educational movement or initiative. Together, they hold the power to impact not only the educational system but an entire society.

This is not a book about building a vision for an idealistic educational utopia. Instead, this book acknowledges the realities and challenges that educators face every day and presents practical strategies for producing real results. In the business world, results typically focus on customer satisfaction, return on investment (ROI), and of course the bottom line. In education, the bottom line is student learning. Realizing an increase in student performance indicators requires a strategic, concerted effort toward instructional improvement. This usually involves teacher professional development.

This book describes a framework for planning and implementing an authentic, job-embedded professional development program for in-service teachers that focuses on incorporating *digital literacies* into the comprehensive curriculum of a school or organization. The framework is modular and highly adaptable in order to meet the unique needs of diverse contexts. It capitalizes on personnel and resources that are already available internally, and it is within reach of anyone who is willing to put the necessary time and effort into implementing it within his or her institution.

This professional learning framework is illustrated in Figure 1.1, but its discussion spans throughout the seven chapters of this book. It may be helpful to refer back to Figure 1.1 regularly in order to gain a clear understanding of the relationship between each of the elements as they are presented.

Before embarking on an in-depth discussion of digital literacies and professional development, let's take a brief look at literacy itself, establish a scope and context for *digital literacies*, and explore some other terms that are becoming increasingly prevalent with regard to literacy in the 21st century.

Figure 1.1   Developing Digital Literacies: A Framework for Professional
              Learning

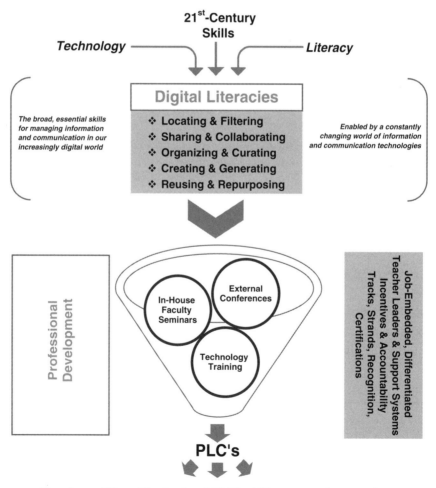

Literacy

At the core of literacy are reading and writing. They are essential tenets of literacy in any society. Any other aspect of literacy builds upon the ability to read and write. However, this just barely scratches the surface. A broader look at literacy reveals that it includes not only reading and writing but truly the ability to engage in *all* types of communication—whether textual, graphical, auditory, or otherwise. Furthermore, literacy involves not just communication but also managing the information that is transmitted by any communication medium. The discernment to choose the appropriate means—whether print, digital, or otherwise—by which to communicate and manage information in a given context is also essential to active citizenship and individual prosperity in a literate society.

A partial and very incomplete list of digital communication mediums might include blogs, text messages, Internet memes, social networks, and multiuser virtual environments (MUVEs). Often overlooked print-based communication formats include comic books, recipes, and appliance service manuals, just to name a few. Indeed, even these items, which have traditionally been available primarily in printed format, are now migrating to the digital realm in the form of web content, e-books, and more.

Surely by now it is apparent that teaching students to read, write, speak, and listen is not nearly sufficient in order to prepare them for success in the highly digital world that is the 21st century.

Defining Digital Literacies

Digital literacies represent in whole the essential skills for managing information and communication in the rapidly changing and increasingly digital world that is the 21st century. The term *digital literacies* is plural (e.g., literacies) because it encompasses a broad spectrum. There is not merely one single digital literacy. Furthermore, *digital* is the most appropriate descriptor because it acknowledges the irrevocable impact that technology has made—and will continue to exert—on literacy. The term *new literacies* is being used increasingly in a similar context to that which is being described here. However, to replace the word *digital* with *new* would risk implying that something might fall off the list at some point when it is no longer on the cutting edge. Any other substitute would only narrow the scope of literacy and further exclude essential elements that cannot be overlooked in a comprehensive treatment of literacy.

I am concerned that there might be a tendency to approach digital literacies from the angle of technology skill acquisition. Teachers and students alike struggle to stay abreast of new technologies and chase frantically as rapid advancements leave them behind. Digital literacies are not merely about gaining new technology skills, learning to use new tools, or even simply applying those tools in teaching and learning. Instead, digital literacies are the highly adaptable skills that actually *enable* us to leverage those technical skill sets and navigate the information superhighway. Rather than locking us into skills and techniques that are relevant now but may change tomorrow, digital literacies make us ready for the present *and* the future, regardless of what it looks like.

> **Digital literacies represent in whole the essential skills for managing information and communication in the rapidly changing and increasingly digital world that is the 21st century.**

Indeed, digital literacies are not static benchmarks that can be arrived at and maintained. The ability to constantly adapt existing skills and develop new ones when appropriate is essential in a rapidly changing society with technologies that are advancing at an unfathomable pace.

Standards

Digital literacies have played a part in the inspiration of numerous sets of standards established by as many experts and professional organizations. The International Society for Technology in Education (ISTE) has its National Educational Technology Standards (NETS) for students, teachers, and administrators. The American Association of School Librarians (AASL) authored its own set of Standards for the 21st Century Learner. The Partnership for 21st Century Skills (P21) supports a Framework for 21st Century Learning. These are just three examples among many more that could be mentioned here.

Subject-matter and discipline-specific organizations often develop standards related to digital literacies (often with slightly different terminology) which complement their content-area standards. All of these can be located easily online, as can pages and pages of search results with blogs, wikis, and articles that attempt to encapsulate digital literacies (again, usually under a different banner) in a list of competencies.

The Digital Literacies

The five digital literacies are expressed as action verbs, which point to methods of managing information and communication of all kinds in any context. They are as follows:

- Locating and Filtering
- Sharing and Collaborating
- Organizing and Curating
- Creating and Generating
- Reusing and Repurposing

Locating and filtering involves finding and identifying resources and paring down those resources in order to arrive at exactly the information that is desired. Digital technologies have enabled *locating and filtering* at a much higher level of accuracy and efficiency than has ever been possible in the past when printed media were the primary means of research and communication. Examples of technologies that form the backbone of *locating and filtering* include Internet search engines, online research databases, and the ability to tag and categorize digital resources.

Sharing and collaborating highlights the social movement that has swept the globe, thanks to the advent of social media and the interactive, collaborative web. Certainly, *sharing and collaborating* has always been an essential element of literacy (even the early cave drawings were a form of sharing information and communicating with others), but it truly encompasses the full range of digital literacies. (Figure 1.2 illustrates the relationships between each of the digital literacies later in this chapter.) A few key technologies that facilitate *sharing and collaborating* include social bookmarking, online document platforms, wikis, blogs, social networks, augmented reality (AR), and multiuser virtual environments (MUVEs).

Organizing and curating involves the recursive process of making orderly sense of resources and content that is otherwise fragmented and scattered. It consists of more than cataloguing or bookmarking; instead, it leads to new meaning and a deeper understanding of information and communications due to the strategic presentation of such material. In terms of Bloom's Taxonomy, *organizing and curating* requires teachers and students to engage in higher order thinking through analysis and evaluation. Technologies pertaining to *organizing and curating* include, but are not limited to, e-portfolios, social bookmarking, blogs, and microblogging.

Creating and generating as digital literacies acknowledges the responsibility that every digital citizen holds as a content contributor in our 21st-century global society. The Internet—and furthermore, social media—have accelerated a movement toward collaborative content creation, thereby resulting in the need for focused attention at a high level within the context of teaching and learning. *Creating and generating* is an excellent example of how digital literacies truly encompass nondigital forms of literacy as well. Indeed, we are *creating and generating* as we write a letter, keep a journal in a spiral notebook, or draw illustrations on paper. In the digital realm, *creating and generating* is facilitated through technologies such as wikis, blogs, podcasts, e-portfolios, augmented reality (AR), and multiuser virtual environments (MUVEs).

Reusing and repurposing has seen its rise, along with advancements in digital technology, as the ability to mashup and remix content from multiple online sources has become a reality. Low-tech versions of this would include fanfiction literature and the work of pop artist Andy Warhol, including his famous Marilyn Monroe pieces. Virtual globes, interactive time lines, and numerous online mashup tools represent a sample of the modern technological tools that enable *reusing and repurposing* as digital literacies.

Table 1.1 summarizes the five digital literacies along with their associated information and communication technologies.

Table 1.1   Digital Literacies and Their Associated Information and Communication Technologies

Digital Literacies	*Information and Communication Technologies*
Locating and Filtering	Internet search, research, tagging
Sharing and Collaborating	Social bookmarking, online document productivity, wikis, blogs, social networking, AR, MUVEs, identity and privacy management, Creative Commons
Organizing and Curating	E-portfolios, social bookmarking, wikis, blogs, microblogging, AR
Creating and Generating	Wikis, blogs, podcasts, e-portfolios, MUVEs, Creative Commons
Reusing and Repurposing	Virtual globes, interactive time lines, mashups, remix, fanfiction

Emergent Literacies

Why *digital literacies*? A variety of terms have emerged in recent years that attempt to expand upon traditional literacy. Digital *literacy* can be recognized as one of those niches; but this book addresses digital *literacies*—and for a very specific reason. That reason will be revealed later in this chapter, but first let's take a quick trip around the block to size up this neighborhood of emergent literacies before we zone in on our home base—*digital literacies*. We will define several other types of literacy and literacies, and in doing so, provide a context within which to situate the concept of digital literacies as it is addressed throughout this book. These emergent literacies include the following types:

- Computer literacy
- Cultural literacy
- Game literacy
- Media literacy
- Multimedia literacy
- Network literacy
- Social literacy
- Visual literacy
- Web literacy
- Multiliteracies
- Information literacy
- New literacies
- Digital literacy

Computer Literacy

Computer literacy refers to the ability to use computers and related technology—such as software and hardware devices—with a certain level of efficiency. Just as competency requirements for any type of literacy are typically defined differently by various entities, so are the exact skills and abilities that are deemed necessary in order to be considered computer literate. Some views of computer literacy focus on software skills related to Microsoft Office and performing basic computer functions. However, a more complete definition of computer literacy acknowledges not just one's ability to operate computers and use specific programs. Instead, it identifies individuals who have the fluency required to learn to use new software and hardware with considerable independence by employing appropriate methods of learning such as hands-on exploration and locating and obtaining relevant learning resources.

It makes sense that an individual's level of computer literacy might be correlated with the degree of hands-on computer experience that he or she is afforded. Those who have access to modern technology—and those who do not—are separated by a so-called *digital divide*. Schools are faced with the challenge of bridging the digital divide in order to instill computer literacies and ultimately digital literacies into their students.

Cultural Literacy

Decades ago when the push for the arts in education began in full force, there was an emphasis on encouraging the development of well-rounded students through exposure to and participation in music, art, theater, and the like. This was an early push for the expansion of traditional literacy—a sort of cultural literacy—much like these other forms of literacy are today in our digital society.

Game Literacy

Individuals who demonstrate game literacy are familiar with the conventions of games and are able to assimilate gaming concepts into otherwise distant contexts, such as academic and professional scenarios. Whereas basic literacy involves decoding and interpreting texts within a broad range of contexts, game literacy encompasses the ability to decode the content of a game and interpret it within the context of human culture, the game itself, other games and genres, and the gaming technology. While discussion of game literacy often focuses on videogames, a more comprehensive definition might also touch on the use of badges and other game mechanics for the gamification of learning and other experiences that would otherwise bear no resemblance to a game.

Media Literacy

Media literacy is first and foremost about being a savvy consumer in terms of how media and marketing messages are received. It is the ability to identify, interpret, and analyze the seemingly endless array of messages conveyed through increasingly diverse media that have become pervasive in today's society. A list of examples could span many pages but would include television commercials, billboards, magazine ads, graphic tees, robocalls, product placement in films, door hangers, and even those sponsored Twitter and Facebook posts that are pinned to the top of your social media feed. While media literacy is primarily about how messages are perceived, it also encompasses the ability to strategically produce and distribute media messages using appropriate channels of communication (and these channels may or may not be digital). The Internet, social networking, and new online niche entrepreneurs have enabled the average citizen to become a media-literate producer by launching YouTube videos that become viral, advertising products through Facebook pages, and having custom T-shirts screen-printed for pennies and posted for sale online at the click of a button.

Media literacy is sometimes discussed in combination with critical literacy, although critical literacy certainly expands beyond the realm of media.

Multimedia Literacy

Multimedia literacy might be used synonymously with media literacy, but multimedia literacy can also be applied with greater specificity to the use of multimedia tools such as video, audio, animation, and slideshows to convey information and manage communication. Too often is the poorly authored slideshow or haphazardly assembled video used in the classroom, on stage, or online to convey otherwise legitimate information to an audience that will be swayed more significantly by the multimedia than by the content. Like so many of the other literacies described in this section, multimedia literacy certainly involves the skilled use of technology tools, but its overarching idea is in *how* those tools are used and the messages that are conveyed and perceived.

Network Literacy

Network literacy in the 21st century recognizes the complex virtual networks which have become so prevalent online. Individuals who develop network literacies are able to identify networks that are relevant to their personal interests and professional activities and engage actively in not only participation but also contribution to the network for the benefit of all members. They have a solid understanding of how these networks form, operate, and evolve over time. Such networks may be formal or informal in nature. Educators often develop personal learning networks (PLN) as a form of professional development. These will be discussed in depth in later chapters. E-mail listservs, online forums, and LinkedIn Groups are also examples of networks that are made possible by the Internet.

Social Literacy

Individuals who possess the characteristics associated with social literacy are able to not only interact but in fact thrive in social environments. This is neither limited to recreational situations nor formal interactions. Indeed, socially literate people are familiar with the diverse cultural and situational norms that might possibly come into play in daily life, both personally and professionally. They are able to make decisions that give respect to all parties involved and engage cooperatively to solve problems and achieve common goals. Social literacy involves collaboration.

With the advent of online social networking, social literacy began to evolve into much more than personal interactions and surface communication. Each type of online social network—and new ones are popping up constantly—is designed to approach social interaction from a unique angle, supposedly filling a purpose not met elsewhere in the virtual realm. With that, there are different shades of social literacy that must be considered when engaging in activity within each of those online environments. Anyone who has spent much time perusing Facebook has surely noticed users and their content that seemingly distort its intended purpose and reflect poorly on the individual. While this happens all the time without drawing great attention, the larger incidents have become the impetus behind new professional ethics policies at the institutional level, targeted legislation from state and federal lawmakers, and a rapidly growing case law. Likewise, users on LinkedIn—a professional networking site—should educate themselves on the unique norms associated with communication and collaboration on that highly targeted site and gain an understanding of how to use the tools and features in a manner that is both professional and productive. Examples like these could be shared for every social network.

Visual Literacy

Visual literacy denotes the ability to draw meaning from visual images of any type—whether print or digital. Some consider visual literacy to be the earliest form of literacy—predating even linguistic literacy (having to do with words)—as the Cro-Magnons drew visual depictions on the walls of caves. Like other literacies, visual literacy is about both receiving and transmitting information. That is, individuals who have a solid grasp on visual literacy are able to not only interpret visualizations but also create visuals to share ideas and knowledge. Just as social literacy has been radically impacted by online technology, so has visual literacy been augmented to include digital media that changes constantly.

Web Literacy

Web literacy is about being an intelligent consumer on the Internet and engaging productively in content creation that contributes to the collective intelligence of the World Wide Web. There are certainly overlaps between web literacy and information literacy. *Indeed, by now it is, no doubt, obvious that each of these emergent literacies intersects with the others in one way or another.* It is vital that users evaluate the accuracy of any and all information found online by considering the authority of the authors, determining how current the resource is, checking for bias, and looking for sources that give a comprehensive treatment of the subject matter.

Web literacy also addresses the importance of online safety and issues such as crime, privacy, and virtual communication (e.g., chat rooms, social networks, e-mail, forums, etc.). It is about the ability to differentiate between legitimate advertisements and scams and recognize when other people are not

> Each of these emergent literacies intersects with the others in one way or another.

who they say they are. Now that the Internet is a pervasive part of everyday life, there is an urgent need for web literacy among all citizens, young and old.

Multiliteracies

Multiliteracies first of all address the need to communicate across cultures, languages, and dialects in our increasingly interconnected world. But a more complete treatment of the term encompasses the type of multimodal communication that has been enabled through modern technologies such as the Internet and mobile devices. Information transmissions and communication events seldom involve just one medium anymore. For example, a single person-to-person interaction facilitated by the use of a smartphone might leverage text, digital graphics, sound, gestures, and tactile interaction simultaneously. A person who can engage in both operating within those communication formats and also decoding their meaning is demonstrating fluency in multiliteracies. While this example involves the use of digital technology, it is important to keep in mind that multiliteracies do not necessarily have to involve a digital component.

Information Literacy

Information literacy describes the acts of locating, interpreting, organizing, and sharing information in such ways that it is meaningful not only to the communicator but also the audiences who are intended to receive the information. It involves applying the correct techniques in order to engage in research. In an age of information overload, it is more important than ever that students become proficient at using appropriate methods of obtaining and transmitting information by locating sources that are both relevant and reliable and then manipulating and disseminating information according to the highest standards of academic integrity and intellectual property. It is worth mentioning here that the Internet is not the only focus of information literacy and neither are print resources. Indeed, mobile technologies and even gaming platforms present avenues of obtaining and transmitting information that demand special attention with regard to literacy development in the 21st century.

Information literacy is often addressed jointly with critical literacy. It is sometimes combined or used interchangeably with communication literacy. Research literacy might be considered a subset of information literacy, and information literacy a subset of computer literacy. Media and information literacies are sometimes paired together within certain contexts.

New Literacies

New literacies is a broader term than many of the others mentioned in this section. It is connected closely to the New Literacies Research Team at the University of Connecticut, which studies the new reading comprehension and learning skills associated with online and other modern technologies. New literacies are also seen through another lens as being reflective of the digitally driven and highly social nature that characterizes all types of 21st-century discourse. In any case, the term places a forward emphasis on the newly emerging implications of literacy in society. Of all the emergent literacies discussed here, new literacies bear the closest resemblance to the digital literacies that form the basis for this book.

Digital Literacy

Digital literacy (notice the singular form of the second word) is often used to refer to the broad ability to work with digital tools and select the appropriate tools to use for a given task. It represents one's preparedness to engage actively within a digital environment. Digital literacy encompasses data management, media objects, and all types of digital manipulation for the purpose of dealing with information and communication. It represents a certain type of literacy that involves digital technology, but its scope is much narrower than that of the *digital literacies* which will be expounded upon in the latter part of this chapter and throughout the book.

Commonalities Among Emergent Literacies

Table 1.2 summarizes the emergent literacies in order to provide an at-a-glance look at these niches of literacy, which both complement

Table 1.2   Emergent Literacies at a Glance

Computer Literacy	The ability to learn and use computers and related technology
Cultural Literacy	A certain level of exposure and familiarity with the creative arts
Game Literacy	Diverse gaming experience and the ability to interpret games in many contexts
Media Literacy	Interpreting all meaning contained within media messages
Multiliteracies	Communication fluency across cultures, societies, and technological modalities
Multimedia Literacy	Using multimedia tools to convey information effectively
Network Literacy	Navigating, interacting, and discerning within virtual and human networks
Social Literacy	Thriving in diverse social contexts, both online and offline
Visual Literacy	Drawing meaning from visual depictions; also, to create such imagery
Web Literacy	Handling content and collaboration safely and productively online
Information Literacy	Locating, interpreting, organizing, and sharing information appropriately
New Literacies	Online reading comprehension and learning skills; social adaptability
Digital Literacy	Working intelligently with digital tools and data

and contrast with digital literacies, as will become evident through-out this book. Consider the following themes, which seem to emerge when exploring a cross section of emergent literacies:

- Fluent literacy involves being both an intelligent *consumer* and a skilled *producer* of information and communication.
- A comprehensive view of literacy pays respect to the long-established information and communication modalities (e.g., pencil and paper, books, etc.) while duly acknowledging those brought forth by the advent of modern and progressive technologies (e.g., texting, virtual worlds, etc.).
- While literacies must at some level include specific skill sets—such as those required for the use of technology tools—*the real emphasis is placed on the ability to learn and adapt on a continual basis as society changes and technology evolves.*
- Decoding and interpreting content varies across contexts, often drastically. Each subset of literacy casts a different light on the tasks involved in managing information and communication, which may otherwise seem similar.
- There is no predominate form of literacy, but there are potentially infinite subsets of literacy. Society and technology largely influence the emergence of new facets of literacy.

The Five Digital Literacies

A brief survey of various emergent literacies provided a bit of *context* as well as some *contrast* with which to situate the digital literacies that are the focus of this book. Indeed, they describe several subsets of literacy and acknowledge many (but not all) of the pieces that fit together as digital literacies. They serve as somewhat of a foundation

> **Digital literacies encompass all of the emergent literacies . . . and more.**

but actually more of a launching point. Put another way, digital literacies encompass all of the emergent literacies just described—and more. But digital literacies are not merely a slice of the pie.

The remainder of this chapter focuses on establishing a conceptual basis for each of the five digital literacies. It begins to touch on how they apply to both teaching and learning and life in general. No doubt, this discussion alone could easily expand to fill many volumes. Figure 1.2 illustrates the relationship between each of the digital literacies and depicts the ways in which the various information and communication technologies can be leveraged for multiple purposes.

Figure 1.2   Understanding the Relationship Between the Digital Literacies

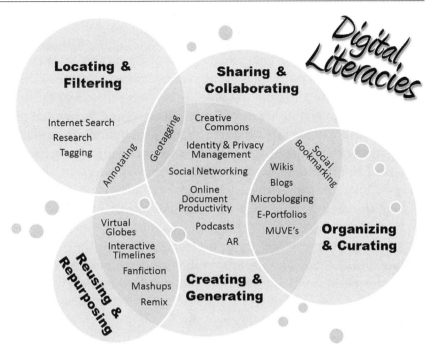

Locating and Filtering

Locating and filtering is a natural starting point for digital literacies as it addresses the task of locating resources and sifting through extraneous content amidst today's state of information overload. It begins as a cognitive disposition—a way of thinking—where a person does not simply default to performing a plain language Google search in order to find something online. Instead, it requires using carefully crafted queries in targeted search engines (which may or may not fall under the umbrella of Google!). Users might call upon a library's web-based research database, a knowledge engine such as Wolfram | Alpha, or perhaps even a printed information resource that is not otherwise available online. Individuals who are skilled at *locating and filtering* know how to employ a high level of critical analysis in order to identify accurate, reliable resources and red flag those that are not. Web-based tagging and annotation tools are harnessed for their power to manage research, share it with others, and make future research easier for everyone. New ways of creatively organizing and displaying information bring learning to life like never before. Individuals feel a sense of social responsibility to contribute actively by collectively managing the vast expanse of information that exists across the web.

Locating and filtering also encompasses geotagging and augmented reality where location awareness melds research and real objects virtually seamlessly thanks to cutting-edge mobile technologies.

Locating and filtering is like taming the web. A good analogy is that of a person panning for treasure at Crater of Diamonds State Park in Murfreesboro, Arkansas. It is touted to be the world's only public diamond mine, and visitors travel for miles and miles in order to sift through acres of soil in hopes of finding a tiny gem. Just as the tourists must have a deliberate strategy in their search for diamonds (such as not sifting the same bit of soil over and over again), so must consumers of information take an intelligent approach to *locating and filtering* (like looking beyond the first page of search results) in order to find the resources that often seem to be that needle in the haystack.

Within the context of teaching and learning, students engage in *locating and filtering* when they select and use appropriate search engines and databases to perform online research and then evaluate both information and information sources for accuracy, relevance, and validity.

Sharing and Collaborating

While digital literacies certainly do not demand a sequential approach, there does seem to be a somewhat logical pathway in terms of how they relate to each other. While *locating and filtering* involves primarily managing information from the consumer's perspective, *sharing and collaborating* brings communication into play and stretches a person to begin exploring the role of a producer of content. *Sharing and collaborating* builds upon the idea of the collective intelligence, where the global knowledge base grows exponentially due to collaboration, cooperation, and competition. This may be both formal and informal in nature. It occurs both naturally and deliberately. *Sharing and collaborating* encompasses the vast realm of social networking but also involves more specific venues like web-based document platforms, e-portfolios, and multiuser virtual environments, just to name a few. And of course, low-tech methods of *sharing and collaborating* should not be overlooked. While they may play a different and possibly lesser role in information and communication management, their persistent existence demands inclusion in this subset of digital literacies known as *sharing and collaborating*. After all, they maintain an irrefutable relationship with other, more digitally driven modalities.

Sharing and collaborating is of utmost importance because it is where identity and privacy management comes into play. The social and web literacies described earlier peek in under this guise as a reminder of the potential dangers presented by the unprecedented ease of sharing and communication now possible, thanks to online and mobile technologies.

Sharing and collaborating online has become part of the 21st-century culture. Businesses feel compelled to leverage as many social networking channels as possible in order to draw the attention of the masses, and individuals feel obliged—or at the very least, pressured by society—to participate in online social communities in order to stay relevant.

As educators, we must abandon the misnomer that our slideshows and other self-developed instructional materials are a sort of private property that should be locked up and protected by a guard dog. Too many teachers claim as their reason for banning students' personal devices in the classroom, the fear of students stealing their intellectual property by recording lectures or capturing images of whiteboard diagrams. The era of open educational resources is here, and educators should be eager to ramp up the global knowledge base—and that of their own students—by this very *sharing and collaborating* that constitutes the second facet of digital literacies. Creative Commons licensing presents a way by which to manage sharing intellectual property while maintaining rights and ownership. More on this in Chapter 7.

In the classroom, students engage in *sharing and collaborating* when they learn together with iPads or interactive whiteboards, connect with authors via Skype, maintain a blog for reflective discourse while reading a short story or novel, or take an interactive virtual field trip.

Organizing and Curating

Organizing and curating can be likened to a neatly arranged spice cabinet. It is like a medley of resources made available within easy reach and situated in a digital array that is both visually pleasing and cognitively intuitive. No, this does not describe a web browser's sidebar with an endless list of chronologically arranged Internet favorites. (By all means, close that pop-out and never expand it again.) Instead, *organizing and curating* picks up where *locating and filtering* left off with regard to taming the wild, wild web. Social bookmarking tools such as Diigo allow users to not only created subject-tagged lists of website bookmarks, but they also enable these lists to be shared with others and enhanced through ongoing collaboration. (Disorganized favorites saved locally do little to benefit a personal user, much less the broader learning community.)

A plethora of new curation platforms are popping up almost daily. Each purports to be a revolutionary venue for organizing, editorializing, and sharing topical web content. Scoop.it, Paper.li, and Bundlr are just three examples. Blogs, wikis, and the already-mentioned e-portfolios also fall into the category of *organizing and curating*.

Curation takes organization to a new level. Curating involves not simply categorizing, grouping, or sharing, but also editorializing, reviewing, rehashing, and even archiving. Historians and scientists have been active curators for ages. Now, the concept of curation has presented itself within the realm of digital literacies and information and communication technologies.

Organizing and curating serves to add additional meaning to information that has been procured through *locating and filtering* and further enhances the benefits that can be reaped by others when such knowledge is disseminated through *sharing and collaborating.*

Students engage in *organizing and curating* when they develop a wiki site profiling the Great Depression, engage in digital storytelling about local culture, or create an Internet radio station with commentary featuring music from the Big Band Era.

Creating and Generating

Creating and generating online content became a reality for everyone with the emergence of the second-generation Internet (often referred to as Web 2.0) where web-based platforms made content creation as easy as desktop word processing. Today, *creating and generating* involves whole new worlds (literally!) of possibility, with virtual worlds such as Second Life, Open Sim, and World of Warcraft, and augmented reality that seamlessly combines digital content and tactile objects in ways that earlier virtual reality technologies cannot begin to touch. Imagine developing a gallery of exact-replica artwork inside a virtual world and inviting actual experts of the field to join students *in-world* for a virtual gallery walk and symposium.

Still, the importance of teachers and students alike engaging in *creating and generating* blogs, wikis, and podcasts should not be undersold. Blogging is a valuable form of reflection and a great way to build writing skills in general. Wikis provide a medium for developing multimedia-rich digital projects. Podcasting allows anyone to develop syndicated media that can be consumed just-in-time and on the go by interested enthusiasts. Never before has it been so easy to become a global broadcaster.

But with opportunity comes great responsibility. The ease of contributing to the online content base means that there will be an inherent tendency to do so without attention to the quality of that content which is being posted online. Therefore, teachers have an urgent call to instill in students the digital literacies of *creating and generating* with the highest level of attention to the means by which such content is generated and contributed to the digital community.

As Figure 1.2 illustrates, *creating and generating* overlaps with all but a few facets of the digital literacies. This further serves to highlight the importance of being a contributing member of society, not only in terms of social responsibility, but also with regard to knowledge at the micro and macro levels. Indeed, 21st-century technologies unlock this potential for everyone.

Students are *creating and generating* as they maintain a class blog with original poetry, produce short podcasts of simple rhythmic improvisations, or create digital flash cards in order to study bird species.

Reusing and Repurposing

Mashups and remix form the basis for *reusing and repurposing*. The concept of taking content and reworking it to serve a new purpose might seem a bit obscure or even out of line. Certainly, this should only be done within the scope of intellectual property rights; but as was mentioned earlier, there is a strong movement toward open source data and open educational resources. Consider the fact that anyone with an intermediate level of technical ability can draw upon the premier online map services in order to develop their own web applications. A large-scale example of this is the metropolitan transportation provider, but there are a multitude of home-grown spinoffs as well. A simpler example of *reusing and repurposing* is the interactive time line that brings together text, images, video, and other media objects into a mashed-up, linear multimedia presentation.

Fanfiction has for some time been a boon for getting young people to write. Fortunately, the Internet has only further enabled fanfiction and remix to flourish. Literary and big-screen sensations such as Star Wars, Lord of the Rings, and The Twilight Saga have inspired enthusiasts of all ages to engage in creative writing and collaborative authorship that represent the epitome of digital literacies. These works of content remix are not limited to only texts but also include graphical anime, video montages, and even Hollywood films. Professional music groups often remix pieces from other musician's work (with permission) in order to create derivative works. There are a variety of motivations behind such actions, including building hype among fans, paying tribute to other well-known figures, and of course, parodies.

Perhaps it is becoming evident how this type of literacy activity can cause online communities to mature beyond casual chat rooms and discussion forums to become a place where intellectual growth occurs and creativity abounds. Much like the salons of the classical era, these digital environments are the birthplaces of new ideas that have the capacity to make a significant impact on society at large. They also represent a means by which to develop literacy skills within the context of teaching and learning.

Students engage in *reusing and repurposing* when they write fanfiction online, create an interactive time line profiling the U.S. Supreme Court Justices, design a digital poster collage with embedded multimedia featuring Impressionist composers, or assemble a video montage that conveys healthy diet and exercise lifestyles.

Memes

One additional concept that deserves mentioning here is the meme—something that has seen a rise along with the growth of the collaborative web. A meme is an idea of some sort that is spread from person to person to the point that it actually becomes a piece of culture. Memes were around long before the dawn of the Internet, but they have taken a new prominence in today's culture in the form of viral videos, image macros (How many different phrases have you seen superimposed on a photo of Willy Wonka?), and of course, web celebrities such as Rebecca Black. Memes are as much a part of digital literacies as the ability to understand clichés in context has always been. Wondering if you have spotted a meme? Find out at http://www.knowyourmeme.com.

Digital Literacies in the Context of Teaching and Learning

The digital literacies are extremely relevant and highly applicable in all grade levels. While the complexity will vary, the tools and strategies are accessible even in the elementary grades. As a complement to the instructional examples described within this book, the companion website (http://www.digitalliteracies.net)

> **Educators often *teach with technology*, which does little to equip students with the skills they need beyond the classroom.**

lists additional ideas and provides links to web sites and tools that support student learning activities leveraging digital literacies.

The purpose of this book is to provide a framework by which educators can systemically integrate digital literacies into teaching and learning—a process which begins with and is supported by teacher professional development. Educators often *teach with technology* as they use document cameras, interactive whiteboards, and web-enhanced project-based learning to facilitate instruction. This, however, does little to equip students with the skills they need beyond the classroom.

Teaching *with* a piece of technology merely demonstrates a device or application, even with hands-on student participation. Teaching students *how to use* a technology tool loads them with skill sets that will likely be obsolete in a short time as technology changes rapidly.

On the other hand, *infusing* digital literacies within the very fabric of content-area instruction will result in authentic learning experiences that not only teach the relevant subject-matter and incorporate 21st-century technology but also address the vital literacy skills that are so strongly emphasized in the Common Core State Standards.

QUESTIONS FOR REFLECTION AND DISCUSSION

1. How does the concept of digital literacies provide a lens through which literacy becomes even more applicable across disciplines than it might seem within the context of a more classical definition of literacy?

2. In what ways can teachers and administrators approach the digital literacies so that the emphasis is placed on real-world relevance rather than merely technology-driven instruction?

3. What are some ways in which each of the five digital literacies can be integrated into the existing curricula immediately, even before beginning an in-depth initiative?

2

Professional Development That (Really) Works

Any systemic change in teaching and learning begins with purposeful and effective teacher professional development. Professional development requires careful *planning, marketing, implementation*, and *follow-up*. The effectiveness of such an initiative can be measured by transfer to classroom instruction and, ultimately, marked increases in student learning outcomes.

There is no miracle treatment for professional development. The educational system is much too complex, and the needs of educators and students are far too diverse for a fix-all solution. There are, however, tools and approaches that can be employed in order to successfully plan and implement a professional development program that is targeted at the unique context of your school or organization. This is the premise of Chapter 2.

Standards

The Standards for Professional Learning, developed by Learning Forward (http://www.learningforward.org), provide an excellent set of standards and descriptors to guide educators as they engage collectively in professional growth activities.

The National Educational Technology Standards (NETS) for administrators, teachers, and students (developed by the International Society for Technology in Education or ISTE)—along with the ISTE NETS Essential Conditions for effectively leveraging technology for learning—provide guidelines and benchmarks for the use of technology in teacher professional development and in classroom instruction.

These sets of standards, combined with the tools and approaches described in this chapter, serve as a solid foundation for creating meaningful, effective professional growth experiences that really make a difference in teaching and learning throughout an institution.

Part One: Characteristics of Effective Professional Development

Why do we have professional development? What is its purpose? Certainly, it aims to improve student performance. Another function is to meet requirements established by state governing bodies in order to maintain teacher licensure. It is intended to expose educators to new methods and resources for teaching and to improve the quality of instruction. Professional development can also be used as a way to develop teacher leaders and facilitate the formation of a professional community of lifelong learners.

In any case, professional development must be given careful treatment in order to ensure meaningful results. Haphazardly planned events are doomed before they start. Adult learning theory—or andragogy—tells us that adults want to know the purpose of instruction. They desire an express understanding of how it relates to the real world and their professions. Adult learners benefit most from practical learning experiences where they are actively involved in meaning-making and able to apply what they learn instantly to their own professional practices. It is important to keep in mind these traits when approaching professional development in a leadership role.

When asked what constitutes good professional development, one teacher put it this way: "Give teachers what they need—when they need it—and then give them the time they need to do it." This pretty much hits the nail on the head, but there's more to be gleaned from this statement than initially meets the eye. I see at least five descriptors that can be drawn from that teacher's valid assessment of what good professional development looks like. Professional development that teachers tend to

> "Give teachers what they need—when they need it—and then give them the time they need to do it."

find most meaningful can be characterized as being *job-embedded, well-planned, differentiated, cohesive,* and *ongoing.*

Job-Embedded

Job-embedded training provides meaningful opportunities for teachers to actually develop materials and implement strategies that meet immediate needs in their instructional contexts. All other characteristics only serve to enhance or detract from the job-embedded nature of professional development. Teachers who participate in job-embedded professional development are able to make an instant connection to the work they are doing in their own classrooms. They find it extremely relevant and timely; and because it is valuable with regards to their own needs, teachers buy into it.

This is in contrast to generic training that is often rather disconnected from what is actually happening in the classroom—or that seems to ignore the widespread needs at hand in classrooms and across the institution. Professional development providers should avoid merely adding another task to teachers' to-do lists and should instead go to great lengths in order to design and implement professional development in such a way that it is job-embedded from the perspectives of *all* stakeholders.

The *closer* training and support are to teachers' primary workflows and the instructional challenge or problem being addressed, the higher the probability that

> The closer training and support are to teachers' primary workflows, . . . the higher the probability that change will occur.

change will occur and have an actual impact on teaching and learning.

Well-Planned

Planning seems like an obvious step in any process. Unfortunately, however, busy administrators and teacher leaders often fail to give enough time and resources to advance planning and preparation. Consider this: *For a faculty of 55, a poorly executed session wastes not just 1 hour . . . but 55 hours!* This should be a wake-up call to anyone involved in professional development leadership. You hold precious time in your hands. Use it wisely!

The impact of well-planned and executed time with faculty can be exponential in everyone's favor. On the other hand, the effects of a failed event are guaranteed to have a ripple effect that is difficult to counteract. And remember, success or failure is measured by both the participants *and* the providers.

Planning for professional development is much like planning for classroom instruction. Indeed, teachers must be viewed as learners. Planning occurs not only prior to a professional development event but also throughout that event and after it concludes. Planning encompasses all other aspects described within this chapter.

Differentiated

Differentiation occurs on many levels and at many points through the planning and implementation of professional development. It is important to consider the unique needs of each teacher who will be participating with regards to various aspects as in the list below:

- prior knowledge
- content area
- instructional environment
- curricular guidelines
- technology proficiencies
- equipment constraints

For instance, veteran teachers are often insulted when they find themselves in a session focusing on the use of graphic organizers as a tool for reading comprehension. Most have incorporated Venn diagrams for many years. Likewise, novice teachers who are a product of present-day teacher education programs may feel like they are back in college when forced to sit through an introduction to Bloom's Revised Taxonomy or a primer on constructing learning objectives. While it is absolutely true that both of these groups of teachers could benefit from a review of any concepts that they may feel they have already mastered, professional development leaders can make big strides by merely explaining the purpose of such sessions and perhaps offering separate sections where the teachers who are already proficient in a given area can engage in more stimulating conversations that take the topic to a higher level.

Band and choir directors and coaches often find themselves most frustrated when it comes to professional development sessions that place a primary emphasis on literacy and math. Once again, it is vital that the *purpose* of these sessions be expressly stated and that leaders strive to make concrete connections with all content areas (music and athletics included). It should not be assumed that teachers will form their own connections with the subject matter being presented. Simply acknowledging the differences in how something will apply across content areas, instructional environments, and diverse curricular guidelines can go a long way in leveraging buy-in among all participants.

When instructional technology is involved, the importance of considering diverse skill levels and the availability of such technology cannot be overstated. Nothing is more frustrating than participating in training for a device or piece of software that is not readily accessible within a teacher's classroom. This also applies to technology that exists in the classroom but is not fully functioning due to lack of maintenance or support.

Skilled users need advanced training that challenges them to stretch what they already know, and beginners need step-by-step, introductory training where leaders guide participants through hands-on experiences with technology that is exactly the same as what they have in their own classrooms. That means that software versions should be the same, interactive whiteboard models should be similar (close enough that they offer the same features), and as much as possible, all buttons and settings should be located in the same place as they will be when teachers start looking for them in their own environments.

In terms of cognitive theory, basic technology training should enable *near transfer* of skills and avoid requiring novice teachers to translate operations between dissimilar contexts. On the other hand, intermediate-to-advanced technology training sessions are the appropriate place to challenge teachers to engage in *far transfer* where they apply skills and strategies to solve more complex problems in diverse instructional contexts.

Differentiation is a challenge in the classroom and is no less of a tall order in teacher professional development. Administrators and teacher leaders are challenged to help teachers set personalized goals that will result in actual instructional improvement. When this is accomplished up front, it can be implemented into the overall program and further reinforced on the long term by instructional coaches and through teacher mentoring.

A needs assessment is an essential tool for planning professional development and especially with regard to differentiation. On the back end of a session or event, a participant evaluation form can solicit invaluable data for making improvements to future efforts. Chapter 3 includes a sample needs assessment and participant evaluation form, both of which can be adapted and used as part of a digital literacies professional development program.

Cohesive and Ongoing

One of the gripes of teachers today is that administrators and the broader governing bodies seem to jump from one emphasis to another—one program to the next—without giving any single effort enough time to produce long-term results. It seems that by the time teachers begin to get accustomed to one way of approaching instruction, it is already time to move on to something else that requires yet another overhaul of the entire curriculum. This is certainly not a problem that is isolated to the field of education, but neither is it justifiable by its widespread prevalence as a mistake made by leadership bodies across the board.

This has led some teachers to become reluctant to invest significant time into any emphasis or initiative, lest their efforts be in vain as the program is scrapped for something new. At the same time, those teachers who *do* in fact spend time and energy developing new skills and instructional materials become demoralized because there is no follow-up and little, if any, accountability. In order for a professional development program to be successful, teachers should be held accountable for the information they receive and the actions they are explicitly directed to take in the classroom. Accountability does not necessarily have to take the form of disciplinary action, but teachers do need to be made aware of clear and functional accountability systems.

Professional development should be cohesive and ongoing. Even disparate topics and sessions can often be grouped into a larger initiative that gives a sense of flow to a series of events that might otherwise seem unrelated. Presemester teacher in-service days can be approached as a large event with many sessions that fall under the umbrella of a theme or initiative. The same can be done with a year-long series of professional development events in order to give a greater purpose to each individual session or meeting.

This is one of the beautiful characteristics of the digital literacies professional development program that this book describes. It is a *cohesive* initiative that involves diverse activities which provide *ongoing* support to teachers in order to realize real results in teaching

> **This is *not* merely a one-shot attempt at teaching teachers to teach differently!**

and learning. It is *not* merely a one-shot attempt at teaching teachers to teach differently!

At the same time, reality necessitates that there are varied topics and issues that must be addressed through professional development, and they will undoubtedly change intermittently and quite frequently present themselves without advance notice. That is why, as Chapter 6 discusses, a deliberate plan for long-term, ongoing support is essential.

Over time, a digital literacies professional development program, for instance, may contract and expand in order to *share the stage* with other emphases; but there is always an element that serves a specific purpose for ensuring a lasting impact on instructional practices and, of course, on student learning.

Common Problems and Pitfalls

Several common problems and pitfalls seem to persist that, when left unaddressed, can hinder successful implementation and limit the results that come out of a professional development event or initiative.

Technical Issues

There is a tendency in technology-related training to place too much emphasis on the technology as a tool without making direct connections to teaching and learning. While teachers cannot be expected to make curricular applications of a technology tool if they are not equipped with the skill sets necessary to operate its basic functions, it is a mistake to assume that learning a new technology skill means knowing how to apply it within instruction. There is a fundamental difference between

- training that teaches the *skills* necessary to operate a piece of hardware or software, and
- training that focuses on *strategies* for leveraging a piece of technology as a tool for teaching and learning within diverse curricular contexts.

In fact, there can—and should—be several levels of both types of technology training.

Too often, schools invest significant capital in technology purchases but fail to provide the necessary professional development. Only the innovators and early adopters manage to come up with ways of using the new *toys* within instruction. Meanwhile, equipment sits unused, and other teachers feel a sense of dissatisfaction and disappointment due to the lack of training and support and their own inability to tackle new technology on their own. A deliberate, proactive training plan can help to avoid this pitfall.

Logistical Issues

Because there are always limited resources in terms of time, personnel, and funding, it is tempting to take a one-size-fits-all approach at professional development. Whether or not technology training is involved, it is essential that professional development be differentiated in order to meet the unique needs of each teacher participant. This is an essential tenet of professional development that is truly job-embedded.

It is past time to abandon the widespread habit of using too much of the lecture/presentation format. In short, it is boring. It fails to engage participants actively in higher order thinking. It caters only to auditory (and possibly visual-spatial) learners, which are said to be among the minority of learners as a whole. Even setting aside Howard Gardner's Theory of Multiple Intelligences, just consider the fact that teachers are accustomed to being active throughout the school day as they teach classes and facilitate student learning. Why, then, would a sit-and-get session—where teachers are stuck dormant in a receiving position—be conducive to professional learning?

On another note, the importance of educational research, learning theories, and developmental psychology cannot be overemphasized. Still, when working with in-service teachers, it is best to place primary emphasis on practical applications and then *support* those assertions with a sprinkling of research, theory, and psychology.

One final logistical issue is that of time sensitivity. Going 1 minute too long beyond the planned time frame can erase all of the good things that were accomplished in an in-service session. A colleague of mine once said with a grin that the best way to run a meeting is to start late, end early, and take a long lunch break. While I recognize the spirit of his expression, I will instead suggest that the most efficient and effective leaders can accomplish the objectives of a meeting within the preestablished time constraints and will monitor and adjust as necessary. Be respectful of everyone's time, and they will return the same courtesy.

Affective Issues

Try to focus on molding the dispositions of teacher participants as opposed to force-feeding them technology features and functionalities. Meanwhile, collectively embrace technology, pedagogy, and content as three inseparable components. Work to cultivate a positive ethos and a culture of professional growth within the teaching faculty.

Market professional development as professional learning *opportunities* with an emphasis on the highly fulfilling opportunities that are in store for teacher participants. *Opportunities* seem much more appealing to people than requirements or expectations.

Table 2.1 summarizes the positive and negative traits described thus far, and Table 2.2 highlights several sample strategies for technology professional development and support. Many of these have come from teachers in the field who were asked to share their views of what professional development should ideally look like.

A Concise, Step-Wise Approach

At the beginning of the chapter, I listed four critical steps in managing professional development of any size or scope. Now that we have explored the positive and negative traits of teacher professional development, let's briefly revisit those steps. Throughout the book, we will continue to build upon and apply them within the context of a digital literacies professional development program.

Planning

Professional development *planning* begins with a needs assessment followed by the development of a targeted program. Planning addresses all subsequent steps in the process.

Marketing

Marketing is an often-overlooked aspect of in-house professional development, but it can mean the difference in success or failure.

Table 2.1   Characteristics of Teacher Professional Development

Desirable	*Undesirable*
Job-embedded	Difficult to connect across disciplines
Well-planned	Sit-and-get, one-way instruction
Differentiated with multiple choices	*One-size-fits-all* sessions
Cohesive programming	Fragmented sessions
Ongoing training and support	One-shot training
Well-defined accountability system	Empty expectations with no follow-up

Table 2.2   Sample Strategies for Technology Professional Development and Support

Make extensive use of the hands-on approach to training.
Offer 3- and 6-hour technology skill set–based training sessions at key points throughout the school year; offer smaller, 1-hour sessions throughout the year as follow-ups and to focus on instructional technology strategies.
Offer concurrent sessions to accommodate multiple skill levels, and let teachers choose based upon their needs and abilities.
Give teachers dedicated time to *play* with new technology in a focused environment.
Incorporate time for teachers to actually set up equipment and input any information that might be required in order to use it (e.g., student data, etc.); don't expect teachers to do this on their own time.
Provide ongoing support to teachers (not merely one-time trainings).
Support should be timely; teachers cannot put their lesson plans on hold when technology fails.
Equip teacher leaders with the time, skills, and resources necessary to be a first point-of-contact for instructional technology support.
Allow teachers to observe other teachers successfully using new technology; this might be incorporated into a peer mentoring program.
Hold teachers accountable for implementing the new skills and strategies.
Maintain the technology; include funds for technology replenishment in long-term budget plans.
During a school-wide implementation of a new technology (e.g., iPads), schedule time approximately once a month for teachers to gather and share challenges and successes.

Marketing involves making a compelling pitch, generating excitement among potential participants, leveraging the buy-in of all stakeholders, realizing actual participation, and finally, laying the groundwork for longevity. Marketing is also the place where incentivizing comes into play. All of this and more is expounded upon in Chapter 5.

Implementation

Implementation is the point where the views of teacher participants really take prominence. If asked, teachers should be able to describe a professional development effort as timely, highly relevant, meaningful, and engaging.

Follow-Up

Follow-up involves considering participant feedback, ensuring programming consistency, establishing ongoing support structures, and maintaining accountability systems, among other things. Professional development so often falls short here. Follow-up is addressed from a different angle in Chapter 4 and then more in depth in Chapter 6.

Part Two: Professional Development Models, Formats, and Approaches

The second part of this chapter surveys various common types of professional development programs and activities and then presents some innovative approaches that are drawn from a multitude of experiences by educators in diverse contexts. Some of the long-used professional development formats need to be revamped to capture the interest of educators. No doubt, this can be true of our classroom teaching, too! In many cases, experienced teachers are tired of seeing the same old agenda, year after year, while on the other hand, certain approaches are simply no longer compatible with the way we prefer to learn and interact as a fast-paced, highly collaborative, digital society. School leaders might also enjoy the chance to refresh the typical elements of professional development that have been used repeatedly for so many years. The purpose of this section is *not* to provide mundane descriptions of the professional development events with which we are already familiar. On the other hand, it would be a mistake to leave classic formats like conferences and workshops completely unaddressed in a chapter about professional development. As we established earlier in the chapter, there are certain essential elements that can make such an event a dynamic learning experience for everyone involved. Let's take a *fresh* look at some of the more common formats and approaches for professional development, giving consideration to new ways of leveraging them for school-wide professional learning.

> Some of the long-used professional development formats need to be revamped to capture the interest of educators.

Conferences

Conferences typically occur on the state, national, and international levels. Many educators have attended regional conferences for many years and missed out on the extremely inspiring and invigorating experience of a conference that is presented on a national or international scale. Limited travel budgets make it difficult for schools to send many teachers to outstanding conference events, and unfortunately, it is often the administrators who end up going to conferences instead. However, there is a renewed emphasis of late in the positive impact that can be achieved by sending small groups of teacher leaders to national conferences instead of administrators alone. Indeed, when approached from the right angle, there can be a ripple effect throughout the faculty in terms of both knowledge and morale when a representative group of teacher leaders attends a conference and then engages in deliberate, ongoing follow-up activities with the at-large faculty upon their return.

To identify potential candidates for a select group, school administrators can issue a request for proposals in order to give interested teachers an opportunity to share how they would disseminate the knowledge gained from attending a particular conference in a way that makes a widespread impact on teaching and learning. Once selected, conference attendees should be expected to slate a more specific—yet still tentative—plan for postconference professional development activities with their faculty and make a firm commitment to follow through with it. A debriefing session following the group's return from the conference can serve as a launching point for the leadership roles they will fill with regard to in-house professional development in the weeks and months ahead.

Within the context of the digital literacies professional development framework described in Chapter 3, teacher leaders who attended a national conference would play key roles in the yearlong digital literacies emphasis that involves, among other things, monthly faculty presentations, Professional Learning Communities (PLC) activities, and peer support structures.

It is important to take a strategic approach to participating in a large-scale conference. In addition to preselecting the most relevant sessions to attend, blogging can be an excellent way to keep a daily learning log. A wiki can be set up for a group of teachers from the same school to post handouts, notes, and reflections in an organized fashion. Many conferences are beginning to establish an official hashtag for use on Twitter and Google+ so that attendees can post quick thoughts and bursts of information before, during, and after the event. This provides for on-the-fly note taking as well as an exciting communication channel. All of these social media formats also allow individuals who are not able to attend the conference to tap into the knowledge stream while the events are still taking place.

It can be easy to approach an exciting conference with great enthusiasm and then return home to the reality of an already-busy schedule, never actually following through with any efforts to *apply* what was learned at the event, much less *disseminate* it to colleagues. This tendency should not, however, deter administrators from sending teachers to such valuable events. Instead, a well-defined plan—combined with a special partnership between teacher leaders and school administrators—can serve to ensure a worthwhile investment and a widespread, long-term impact on teaching and learning throughout the institution.

Virtual Conferences

Recent statistics show that most teachers still prefer face-to-face professional development. But there is clearly a growing enthusiasm for virtual events—thus, the increasing number of online conferences that are appearing each year, either as stand-alone events or as complements to already-established face-to-face conferences.

Virtual conferences eliminate the need for expensive travel, although most still require a registration fee in order to cover the expenses of administering the event in terms of personnel, time, and technology resources. A virtual conference can be very cheap to put on, or it can be extremely expensive. When the event involves live video streaming of sessions occurring at a face-to-face conference, high-end equipment and large amounts of bandwidth must be purchased. This can be accomplished in-house by an individual school for a reasonable price; but at a convention center, such resources are of a commercial grade (e.g., broadcast cameras and T1 Internet lines) and therefore, are typically quite costly.

Virtual conferences expand the audience size and geographic reach of an event. Oftentimes, a group of people will gather around a projected computer screen in order to view the virtual conference sessions using a single connection. This is a real advantage to the virtual conference format, and most conference sponsors actually encourage this approach to participation.

One of the drawbacks to attending a conference through an online portal is the fact that not all sessions are typically made available online. Furthermore, networking opportunities are limited unless the conference organizer establishes social networking opportunities such as through Edmodo, Twitter, Ning, or a customized platform. Also, virtual conference participants will miss the time typically spent meandering through aisles of corporate showcases in the always-popular exhibit halls. Perhaps virtual exhibit halls are the next big step in the virtual conference format. Indeed, augmented reality and multiuser virtual worlds already make this a possibility to some extent.

Virtual conferences can run simultaneously with a face-to-face conference. EDUCAUSE uses this approach. Alternately, virtual conferences can be held at different points throughout the year in order to supplement or augment the primary, face-to-face event. Florida Educational Technology Conference (FETC) is one example. Some conference organizers will choose to make these intermittent virtual events available exclusively to those people who paid to attend the face-to-face conference, while others will open them up to anyone for a separate registration fee. Still, others will offer the virtual events for free as a way to generate interest and leverage a larger participation at the face-to-face conference.

Another way to approach the virtual conference is as an asynchronous initiative and a way for experts to share their knowledge, research, and best practices without themselves having to travel to an on-ground event. The Ubiquitous Learning Institute is one organization that offers this option as a part of their annual conference. On their request for proposals, they state clearly that the virtual format holds the same professional credibility and level of achievement as does presenting a paper or facilitating a workshop face-to-face. They aim to dispel any misconception that a virtual presentation might be less respected in curriculum vitae or professional portfolios. Instead of making heavy use of live streaming, papers and other materials are posted on the conference website. In some cases, presenters may be offered the opportunity to record a brief video presentation to be posted alongside the other materials. It is efforts like this one that will further strengthen the legitimacy of virtual learning experiences for professional educators.

The Global Education Conference is an example of an online-only conference, in that it does not have a face-to-face counterpart. It is held annually over the span of several days and captures a global audience. Online-only conferences can establish and maintain a reputation as high-quality, scholarly events by leveraging multiple rounds of RFPs and strategically targeting the right audiences for participation at all levels.

A final type of virtual conference to mention here is that which is held within a 3D virtual world such as Second Life. The Virtual Worlds Best Practices in Education Conference is an outstanding example of such an event. Fortunately, interested participants need not be experienced users of virtual worlds in order to take advantage of these unique professional development experiences. Virtual worlds offer an immersive environment for learning and exchanging ideas and capitalize on the sense of social presence that comes with interacting with other people through avatars in unique, situated contexts. In addition to the innovative work being done by educators, the health care field has broken new ground recently by holding interactive conferences and training events for surgeons and other health care providers in virtual worlds such as Second Life where they can simulate operations and other procedures in contexts that are amazingly near authentic.

> **Virtual conferences can be a value-packed approach for involving as many educators as possible in a high-quality, national event.**

Virtual conferences can be a value-packed approach for involving as many educators as possible in a high-quality, national event. However, they should not be considered to be an equal substitute for attending an event in person.

Seminars

Seminars are often held at a regional, state, or national level. They typically involve a series of breakout sessions and may or may not feature a keynote speaker. Seminars tend to be more focused in terms of content than conferences, and they may not include elements such as exhibit halls, online components, and social activities. They sometimes have a specific audience as opposed to being open to anyone who wants to register to attend. Program development is often executed internally from start to finish without an RFP. These events may offer a lower registration cost since they are on a smaller scale in relation to most conference-type events. It is worth mentioning that single-session events are sometimes referred to as seminars. Indeed, the terminology described throughout this section is used interchangeably at times.

Workshops

The title of workshop implies a significant element of hands-on participation by attendees. Workshops tend to involve training in a specific technology skill, instructional strategy, or series of learning activities. Hands-on workshops demand a great deal of planning and careful execution by facilitators. Participants should be guided through activities by a combination of verbal instruction, printed materials, and collaboration. Step-by-step tutorials, templates, and supplementary materials can be very helpful both during the event and afterward when participants return to their homes and classrooms and begin to apply what they learned in their own contexts.

Hands-on technology workshops are a highly requested format by teachers across the board who are thirsty for more instructional technology support as they are given new software and equipment and expected to implement them within their curricula. However, too many workshops are quick, one-shot attempts at training a large group of teachers. A better approach is to plan series of workshops—each of which lasts 1 to 3 hours—over a long period of time and offer multiple tracks based upon teachers' varying skill levels. For instance, the first part of a workshop series might take place in August during pre-school professional development days, followed by intermittent workshops spread through the school year both on weekdays after school and during student-release days that are dedicated to professional development.

Presentations

Presentations represent the most common format of an in-house professional development session. They may stand alone as their own independent session or be a part of a workshop or other larger event. Presentations should not be mistaken for faculty meetings that are intended solely for administrative dissemination of information. In addition to in-house presentations, teachers often participate in presentations given within the community or at a regional educational cooperative. Presentations have made the slideshow famous. On the other hand, slideshows have given the presentation format a bad rap. Table 2.3 lists and describes five basic principles of designing slideshows for use in a live presentation. Of course, the list could easily double to address other elements such as design style and specific ways to approach content. Also, the principles are somewhat different when a slideshow is intended for use as a stand-alone learning object.

The most effective presentations are situated within a session that engages participants in active learning. Such a session might include all of the following elements in sequence (Summey, 2013):

1. Direct Instruction
2. Multimedia

Table 2.3   Principles of Slideshow Design

Principle	*Explanation*
Focus on content	Start with a topical presentation content outline (not by selecting a presentation design theme)
Let the slideshow *support* the presentation	Use a slide for every topic and subtopic (but not necessarily each *point*)
Be concise	Avoid bullet points and thick paragraphs of text (remember Guy Kawasaki's 10/20/30 Rule)
Convey the big picture	Display data using visual representations (e.g., charts, graphs, infographics)
Use visual metaphors	Use the Creative Commons filter to search Flickr, purchase images from stock photo sites, or take your own photos (sometimes that is the quickest route)

3. Small-Group Discussion

4. Self-Reflection

5. Extension

While too many in-service sessions weigh heavily on direct instruction, a modest amount of presentation-style delivery can be very effective at conveying information and ideas.

This can be enhanced and augmented through the use of multimedia. Certainly, PowerPoint slideshows are the most popular form of multimedia, but videos, animations, websites, simulations, and other types of multimedia—such as those which involve participant interaction through their mobile devices—can really serve to make professional learning experiences dynamic and engaging.

It is important to avoid relying too heavily on multimedia resources because technology sometimes fails and a presenter must be able to proceed without it if necessary. It has been said by those who frequently make presentations that the question is not *if* there will be a technology glitch but *when* and *what*. I was impressed by Seth Godin at EDUCAUSE 2011 when, during his keynote, his slideshow crashed and he reacted ever so smoothly. Fortunately, he was able to reload and fire off the slideshow in a split second. However, he was prepared to proceed without it if necessary, and the way in which he handled that incident—no sense of surprise or frantic reaction—left no doubt in my mind of that fact.

As a presenter or session facilitator, it can be difficult to turn loose of the reins and take the somewhat risky step of directing participants to engage in small-group discussion and self-reflection. These activities require as much planning as a lecture and certainly more intricate facilitation. Still, they can produce incredible results in terms of transfer to the classroom. In fact, participants often say in retrospect that such time is the most valuable part of a session. They request this immediate *application time* more than anything else with regard to the actual time spent in session.

Finally, ensuring that a professional development event—whether one session or a series—results in a lasting impact on teaching and learning requires that there be an extension of that event where teachers apply what they learned and share with colleagues about their experiences. There are numerous ways in which this can be accomplished, but it reflects the *ongoing* nature of professional development that has already been mentioned earlier in this chapter and will be discussed again in Chapter 6.

Professional Learning Communities

Professional learning communities (PLCs) are a mechanism by which teachers are brought together as learners within subcommunities within an entire faculty. PLCs may be formed within or across subject areas and should always be strategically grouped. Within the context of a digital literacies professional development program, it is important that a teacher with strong technology skills be placed in each PLC to serve as a *tech leader* in cooperation with the primary leader of each PLC. (More on this in Chapters 3 and 4.) Oftentimes, administrators will designate a teacher who is certified by the National Board for Professional Teaching Standards as the main leader of each PLC. PLCs provide a structure where teachers can become owners of their concerted professional development. PLCs eliminate teacher isolation. They are a place where teachers can reflect upon their instructional practices and collaborate at every level. PLCs should have a deliberate structure, a purpose, and an action plan. Each member should have a hand in accomplishing the established objectives and be held accountable on both an individual and group level. PLCs have proven to be an extremely successful model of professional development in 21st-century schools. Moreover, they lend themselves quite well to serving as a significant

> **PLCs have proven to be an extremely successful model of professional development in 21st-century schools.**

piece of a larger, multifaceted professional development initiative, such as the digital literacies program described throughout this book.

Peer Mentoring

Peer mentoring can range from informal pairs where support is called upon and provided on an as-needed basis to more structured pairings where rubrics are used, data is collected, and reports are generated. Whatever the structure may be, it is imperative that peer mentoring be a formative and nonthreatening effort and that such evidence of teaching style and ability as is collected during discussions and observations not be reviewed by administrators for evaluation of any sort. To do so would compromise the intended purpose of providing just-in-time support and dealing with instructional issues that a teacher might otherwise be inclined to sweep under the rug when being formally evaluated. Also, faculty should always be actively involved in selecting peer mentors. Administrators who simply assign mentors are setting the stage for failure.

Self-Directed Activities

Independent, self-directed professional development can take many different forms, including, but not limited to, the following examples:

- A book study where a summary and reflection are written and submitted as evidence of professional growth
- College coursework for the purpose of earning an advanced degree, gaining a new professional credential, adding an additional area of certification, or simply taking a course in instructional improvement for its own sake
- Engaging in scholarly research, either individually or in collaboration with one or more colleagues, in order to contribute to the field of education and/or a subject-area
- Fieldwork where data is collected or perhaps service learning is involved
- Curriculum development, especially when multiple teachers collaborate in order to improve upon an existing curriculum
- A Personal Learning Network (PLN), where a teacher leverages social media in order to gain new knowledge, resources, and strategies from experts around the globe through blogs,

podcasts, tweeting, and other types of social journalism. A fully functioning PLN involves the teacher making regular *contributions* to the collective intelligence as well, as opposed to merely being a consumer. A sample PLN is described in Chapter 3.

School administrators should collaborate with library media specialists in order to build up a professional development library with useful, authoritative books that address theory, research, and professional practice. This library should be made easily accessible, with new books added monthly. The professional development library and its growing collections should be advertised regularly in order to maintain prominence as valuable resources for professional improvement.

Creative Approaches to In-House Professional Development

As educators strive to reinvent professional learning in response to widespread cries for reform, a myriad of new ideas have emerged which hold the potential to revolutionize professional development from all perspectives. These are creative approaches that present opportunities for new incentives and leverage motivation through authenticity and convenience. No doubt, there is a subset of practitioners to whom these ideas are old hat, having been forward thinking enough to leverage these angles many years ago. For everyone else, these come as fresh ideas that can serve as a launching point for a highly customized professional development program that fits within the unique context of a school or organization. These models and approaches can best be used in combination with the creative strategies for leveraging buy-in and participation that are explored in Chapter 5.

> **New professional development models tend to leverage motivation through authenticity and convenience.**

Summer Academy

Summer is a great time for teachers to focus on professional development. It is the time of year when school travel budgets empty out and personal resources are tapped as teachers and administrators alike head out in all directions for conferences and seminars. However, summertime also presents an excellent opportunity to offer an in-house academy or institute where a plethora of workshops and seminars can be offered for professional development credit. A summer academy provides a venue for local teachers to serve as session leaders while outside experts are also brought in for specific, big-impact events (much like keynotes at a large-scale conference). Program planners might also consider leveraging partnerships with other school systems by inviting their teachers and administrators to participate as presenters and/or attendees. Such an initiative could potentially grow into a regional event!

An in-house professional development academy is a large undertaking that may involve as much as a full summer of programming. It is important to have realistic expectations about teacher participation and to plan accordingly. On the other hand, schools that customarily plan several days of professional development prior to the start of the school year can recast that time with this new approach and then gradually expand it from there. Organizers might arrange for local companies to provide lunch or other incentives and promotional materials on key days as a way of advertising their products and services while also showing bidirectional community appreciation.

Miniconference

The miniconference format fits well into those student-release days designated for professional development that are often scattered throughout the school year. An event like this provides a certain cohesiveness that does not otherwise exist. A sense of expectation and enthusiasm forms after a successful inaugural iteration of a miniconference—in much of the same way students find themselves anticipating a field trip that has generated hype in previous years. (Have you ever before likened professional development to a field trip?!)

A miniconference should kickoff with an inspiring keynote that really sparks teachers' interests and might include anywhere between two and six breakout sessions, depending upon whether it spans an entire day or just part of one. The importance of incorporating participant collaboration cannot be overstated. Any of these types of events can be ruined by a series of sit-and-get presentations. The point here is not to simply rebrand the same old practices but instead to wipe the slate clean and reapproach afresh and anew.

Also of utmost importance is the need for choice. Each timeslot should offer at least two session options for teachers to choose from. This is huge. Teachers also indicate repeatedly their desire for dedicated work time where they can immediately apply what they have just learned to their own instructional needs. This is a vital element that should be incorporated into any event, regardless of its length or format.

Unconference

An unconference is an increasingly popular term used to describe an event that aims to redefine the traditional conference format. There is no single accepted way to approach an unconference, but one of the most common traits involves the way in which the program is established. With this approach, participants at-large are encouraged to come prepared to present and are given the opportunity to submit one or two proposed topics in a public venue (e.g., sticky notes on a whiteboard) at the beginning of the event. Event organizers then take those proposed topics and quickly organize them into a schedule. They compare the number of participants with the number of topics proposed in order to determine how many sessions will be offered within the preestablished timeslots. Unconference sessions are highly collaborative and emphasize group discussion over lengthy presentations. The casual, on-the-fly nature of an unconference is catching on in particular within the realm of educational technology enthusiasts. One high-quality example is EdCamp, an initiative that has spread across the globe, with well over 100 unconference-style events held worldwide (though mostly in the United States) since the inaugural event in 2010.

The unconference format breaks down the invisible wall between presenters and attendees, giving all participants ownership in the event and making it possible for individuals to share their knowledge and expertise to an eager crowd whereas they might not otherwise find the opportunity to lead a session at a formal conference. Schools can easily apply this model within a single day or even an event that spans multiple days if the pool of faculty participants is large enough to provide a sufficient number of presenters while still offering multiple sessions to pick from during each time slot. Again, keep in mind that professional development events should provide teachers with choices as opposed to requiring everyone to participate in a linear series of sessions. The idea of teachers presenting their own impromptu sessions will likely be met with hesitation during a school's first attempt at an in-house unconference. However, a little encouragement and a lot of initial facilitation by teacher leaders *within the faculty* can help this innovative model gain momentum to the point that teachers will be eager to participate and will actually look forward with great anticipation to the next unconference event.

After-School Cohorts

Teachers tend to dread after-school meetings because they fall at the end of an already-taxing workday, and their to-do lists are spilling over with items that have arisen throughout the day. However, some teachers still prefer to engage in professional development activities after 3:00 p.m., so it is certainly worth keeping the option on the table. One approach is to survey teachers in order to gauge interest and then ask teachers to sign up voluntarily to participate in an after-school cohort group. The key words here are *voluntary commitment*. Indeed, this type of professional development is best billed as voluntary, but if leaders are going to put time and resources into providing such programming, then it is important to have a commitment from a solid group of teachers. An after-school cohort might meet for an hour-and-a-half to two hours in order to allow for substantial progress while not going too late into the evening. Depending on the scope of the content, a cohort might meet as little as three times within a few weeks or as much as 15 times spread throughout an entire school year. These sessions should be hands-on and highly interactive with instant applicability to the teachers' own instructional contexts. By all means, this time should not be filled with one-way presentations.

Here is a quick note, inspired by midafternoon exhaustion and Maslow's Hierarchy of Needs: Since the cohort group is comprised of a consistent roster of participants who will be meeting together regularly, each person might take a turn bringing a snack for the group. Alternately, the school could provide light refreshments. In any case, having something available at the beginning of each after-school cohort session will encourage hungry teachers to skip their run to the nearby drive-through and instead arrive promptly so that the session can begin early and avoid going too far into the evening.

Lunch-n-Learn/Prep-Period Tune-Ups

The notion of offering professional development during that precious hour (or less) during the day when teachers have a moment alone may seem absurd. Nonetheless, it can serve to meet the needs of yet another subset of the faculty who would actually prefer this arrangement due to complicated schedules and other issues that conflict with typical professional development offerings. Furthermore, this type of stop-in event can be invaluable for teachers who need just-in-time assistance with a new technology tool that has recently been implemented (for instance, in schools that are in the middle of 1:1 iPad programs or district-wide SMART Board installations). If professional development providers can stay in tune with the pulse of the faculty and provide sessions that are relevant and timely to the specific needs of the moment, then this format can be a boon for making a difference at the grassroots level. Session facilitators might only see one or two participants at a time, but some valuable hands-on assistance can be provided in this way.

It may be difficult for teachers to facilitate these sessions during the school day unless they have extra release time in order to compensate for their leadership role. Therefore, lunch-n-learns and prep-period tune-ups may fall to instructional coaches, technology staff, and administrators. Still, these bite-sized sessions can make a big impact over time when approached the right way.

Webinars

Webinars are online seminars or web conferences that typically include streaming video and audio. Webinars often incorporate a slideshow-supported presentation followed by a Q&A session. Skype, WebEx, Adobe Connect, and Blackboard Collaborate are just four examples among a long list of web conferencing platforms. One of the great features of a webinar is the ability to record a live session and make it available for playback at a later time. Contrary to what might be expected, participant engagement can be leveraged at an extremely high level with the use of interactive tools such as virtual whiteboards, audience polling, and breakout rooms.

The anytime-anywhere connectivity of webinars is not a license for school leaders to let professional development bleed over into teachers' personal time. However, webinars can serve as yet another avenue by which to differentiate professional development offerings in order to accommodate diverse learning preferences and increasingly demanding schedules.

Online/On-Demand (On-Your-Own)

On-demand professional development might be compared to an Individualized Educational Program or IEP (minus the tedious paperwork). Teachers can determine exactly which of the offerings meet their unique needs in terms of learning styles and professional growth. While there are a growing number of on-demand professional development libraries available for purchase on an individual or subscription basis, another option is to develop in-house materials.

Web-based tools such as Screencast-O-Matic make it extremely easy to develop narrated videos that present a particular topic, tool, or instructional strategy. Another option is TechSmith's Camtasia, which is a piece of software that includes additional capabilities beyond the features included in similar web tools. Finally, Adobe Captivate is a professional grade software package that can be used to create multimedia learning objects that include high levels of interactivity, quizzes, and response-based feedback.

There are a variety of approaches to developing an in-house digital professional development library. Content creators might include administrators, instructional coaches, technology specialists, teachers, and even students. Developing a new digital learning object is not dissimilar to planning and leading a face-to-face workshop, although it is important to understand the large amount of time that is required to develop even a short instructional video clip. These things don't exactly throw themselves together!

Podcasts

One approach is to develop a series of *podcasts* that follow a singular theme. A podcast is a syndicated program with multiple episodes. A single stand-alone video clip is not necessarily a podcast. Embarking upon a podcast project requires a long-term commitment if it is indeed to be a true podcast. In terms of professional development, one of the potential benefits of developing a podcast series is the ability to attract teachers over a long period of time—much like a primetime sitcom might draw you to the TV every Thursday night, for instance.

Learning Bursts

Another approach to online professional development is known as a *learning burst*. Learning bursts are short video clips that resemble a talk show and—like other formats—address a focused topic. They are often accompanied by a worksheet or booklet that engages the learner in higher order thinking, requiring him or her to make applications within the context of professional practice. Learning bursts do not necessarily have to be connected to any sort of series, making them an excellent option in the early stages of assembling a digital content library.

Teachlets

One final format to mention here is the *teachlet*. The defining characteristic of a teachlet is multimedia interactivity. While podcasts and learning bursts are typically playback-only video/audio clips, teachlets engage the learner in some degree of response and customized feedback. This may be in the form of quizzes, simulations, or tutorials. Oftentimes, learners are given the ability to select from multiple pathways within the flow of content presentation based upon level of expertise or preferred learning style. Adobe Captivate is a robust software solution for creating teachlets and similar types of multimedia learning objects. Articulate Studio is a suite of eLearning development tools that offer similar functionalities. Adobe Presenter is an example of a specialized tool that integrates with Microsoft PowerPoint in order to add quizzes and other forms of user interactivity to slideshows. Basic screencasting tools do not typically include options for interactivity.

Hosting Content

A simple solution for making digital video content available for teachers is to set up a channel on a video sharing site such as YouTube or SchoolTube. Also, several of the screencasting tools offer hosting space with various features such as the ability to create multiple embeddable playlists and track usage. However, many of these sites do not support interactive multimedia content such as the Flash files and executables that are generated from Adobe Captivate and the Articulate programs.

When a more flexible solution is necessary, it might be appropriate to set up a wiki or use a website creation tool to develop some sort of web presence that will serve up the podcasts, learning bursts, teachlets, and other digital content that comprise an online professional development library.

On the other hand, when planning the development of a long-term, scalable online professional development resource, it may make sense to leverage the power of a learning management system (LMS). Fortunately, there are a variety of alternatives to costly platforms such as Blackboard and Desire2Learn. CourseSites, a free version of Blackboard, allows users to create a limited number of courses to use for any purpose. While CourseSites's familiar interface may be appealing to people who are accustomed to working with Blackboard, its limited scalability may pose a hindrance to program growth.

> **When developing a long-term, scalable online professional development resource, it may make sense to use a learning management system (LMS).**

Moodle is a popular open source LMS that can be downloaded for free and hosted on a local server. Schools that don't want to deal with local hosting can opt to pay a very reasonable price for remote Moodle hosting by services such as Moodlerooms or Remote-Learner. The potential benefits of using an LMS to offer online professional development are endless. An LMS such as Moodle will allow the creation and use of learning modules, multiple forms of assessment, and a myriad of collaborative elements including integrated social media. Detailed user tracking capabilities make it possible to document activity in ways that the previously mentioned approaches cannot. While the LMS is often looked upon as a tool for use with students, it can be a boon for school leaders who are looking to capitalize on the online delivery method for professional development.

Mobile Learning (On-the-Go)

Pervasive mobile technology in today's society is bringing rise to a new genre of *mobile learning* experiences whereby learners access information and apply knowledge just-in-time, on-the-go, and in contexts which are authentic and situated. According to statistical data, most teachers will possess a mobile phone—many of them smartphones—and an increasing number of schools across the nation are equipping administrators, teachers, and students with iPads for use in teaching and learning.

The personal nature of mobile devices means that teachers can use their own phones and tablets throughout professional development experiences, as opposed to the fragmentation and disconnects that so often occur between training environments and the classroom. This device consistency enables teachers to more successfully transfer learned knowledge and strategies to actual teaching within their own classrooms.

Mobile devices present opportunities for participant response and collaboration in conferences, workshops, and presentations. However, greater potential can be realized through diverse forms of independent mobile learning as the following list demonstrates:

- Accessing reference materials just-in-time, right at the point of need
- Reading e-books for instructional improvement
- Collecting and manipulating data during field-based activities
- Videoconferencing with colleagues and experts in the field
- Connecting to a teacher's computer remotely in order to provide and/or receive technical support

- Collaborating on curriculum development through web-based document platforms
- Leveraging the usefulness of mobile apps for teaching, learning, and professional learning in general
- Participating in a PLN, which might include social media and other forms of information and communication technologies (ICT)

Since mobile learning is often informal in nature, it can be difficult for teachers to provide typical forms of documentation that might be expected in order to receive credit for professional development to count toward annual requirements. On the other hand, some learning management system (LMS) platforms, including Moodle, can be configured to allow mobile access and would then be able to track teachers' activities when facilitated within the LMS. Still, mobile learning is not intended to be forced into such a structured format that it defeats the very purpose of being timely and convenient.

Conclusion

Professional development can be a dynamic, engaging experience for everyone involved when it targets the specific needs of each educator through well-planned, differentiated training that is job-embedded, cohesive, and ongoing in nature. School leaders are encouraged to overhaul long-standing in-service routines and capitalize upon fresh approaches to professional learning—such as those listed in Table 2.4 and described in the second part of this chapter—which will incite a new enthusiasm for instructional improvement within teachers school wide.

Motivation was intentionally left largely unaddressed in this chapter because it is given special attention later on. Chapter 5 presents ideas for motivating teachers to participate, including creative ways to offer financial incentives without having to find new budget money.

Chapter 3 brings together digital literacies and professional development in order to establish an integrated framework for developing a comprehensive program that aims to infuse ICT into the very fabric of teaching and learning. This is not a typical approach to teaching with technology. Chapter 3 gets to the core of *Developing Digital Literacies*.

Table 2.4 Modes of Professional Learning

Common Professional Development Models and Approaches	Creative Approaches to In-House Professional Development
Conferences	Summer academy
Virtual conferences	Miniconference
Seminars	Unconference
Workshops	After-school cohorts
Presentations	Lunch-n-learn / prep-period tune-ups
Professional learning communities	Webinars
Peer mentoring	On-your-own / online / on-demand
Self-directed activities (book studies, PLN, etc.)	On-the-go / mobile

QUESTIONS FOR REFLECTION AND DISCUSSION

1. What unique challenges might be associated with providing professional development that is job-embedded, well-planned, differentiated, cohesive, and ongoing?

2. Identify some problems or issues that characterize current or previous attempts at in-house professional development. How might those concerns be addressed at various levels?

3. Which models or approaches seem on initial consideration to be ideal candidates for developing an in-house professional development initiative that equips teachers to infuse the digital literacies into teaching and learning?

3

A Framework for Program Development and Implementation

Aprofessional development program designed to support the integration of digital literacies into teaching and learning should be comprehensive and ongoing. The program should incorporate elements of differentiation because *teachers* as learners are much like their *student* learners—they have a variety of learning style needs and preferences, and they possess differing levels of prior knowledge.

As Chapter 1 established, digital literacies are the essential skills for managing information and communication in the rapidly changing and increasingly digital world that is the 21st century. Table 3.1 lists the set of digital literacies that is adopted throughout this book. This list was established in Chapter 1 and framed by an examination of digital literacies as it is defined by various contexts, disciplines, and professional organizations as well as its implications in teaching and learning. Along with those digital literacies, Table 3.1 also contains the most relevant examples of corresponding information and communication technologies. These technologies represent the mediums through which people engage digital literacies. Their use in teaching and learning—and in real-world contexts—is addressed in depth in Chapter 7.

Table 3.1 Digital Literacies and Their Associated Information and Communication Technologies

Digital Literacies	Information and Communication Technologies
Locating and Filtering	Internet search, research, tagging
Sharing and Collaborating	Social bookmarking, online document productivity, wikis, blogs, social networking, AR, MUVEs, identity and privacy management, Creative Commons
Organizing and Curating	E-portfolios, social bookmarking, blogs, microblogging, AR
Creating and Generating	Wikis, blogs, podcasts, e-portfolios, MUVEs, Creative Commons
Reusing and Repurposing	Virtual globes, interactive time lines, mashups, remix, fanfiction

Schools can adopt this list of digital literacies or adapt them as needed. They may potentially choose to segment an individual literacy into multiple competencies in order to go more in depth. Alternately, they might prioritize the list and simply omit one or more literacies due to time constraints. Indeed, it is important to adapt as necessary.

Merely glossing over a large number of concepts in too short a period of time is futile. Teachers need ample time to gain a solid understanding and make applications in the classroom.

The digital literacies should be used recursively throughout all aspects of the professional development program:

- Through modeling when leaders disseminate new information to the faculty
- In professional learning communities (PLCs) as teachers collaborate, plan, and reflect
- Within student-centered instructional activities where students actively learn and apply new knowledge and skills in authentic contexts through the use of modern information and communication technologies

In terms of revolutionizing instruction, Marc Prensky (2005) framed it well in an article he wrote for Edutopia. He explains that teachers must stop *dabbling* with technology and move beyond merely doing old things in old ways or even doing old things in new ways. Indeed, they must ultimately do *new* things in *new* ways.

Assigning students to write essays individually using a word processing application would be considered using technology to do old things old ways. On the other hand, teaching students to use an online collaborative document platform such as Google Docs in order to engage in peer editing with students who are separated by time and space would be an example of applying digital literacies skills to engage in collaboration and learning support for the purpose of creating and organizing content.

There are a variety of formats and time lines that can be adopted for implementing a professional development program on digital literacies. Professional development often takes the form of full-faculty meetings, PLCs, peer mentoring, and self-directed study. Scheduled events are most often held after school or as daylong series on student-release days. Indeed, there are other approaches, too, such as sending select faculty and administrators to conferences with the charge of returning to disseminate newly acquired knowledge among the faculty.

While these formats are most effective when used in concert, the reality of many situations will likely necessitate the use of a select number of them in order to accomplish established goals with limited time and resources. Of course, the first step is determining exactly what those goals are. This is where the needs assessment comes into play.

Needs Assessment

Any comprehensive professional development program that includes more than a few haphazard presentations and hopes to achieve meaningful results should be carefully planned and deliberately executed. Such efforts serve to ensure that precious time invested by administrators, faculty, and students is not only worthwhile but also fruitful. Just as teachers are taught to establish learning objectives that guide lesson planning, professional development leaders should likewise begin with the end in mind. Of course, in the broadest sense, the goal is increased student learning; but more specifically, each school should identify its own set of goals that wrap around the idea of students applying digital literacies in authentic, real-world situations.

The needs assessment is an essential first step in planning and implementing any program that hopes to have a purposeful impact. It is vital in order to gain a clear understanding of what is being done currently and subsequently establish goals and determine an action plan for accomplishing those goals. Too often in school systems, teachers are left out of the planning process and administrators set goals without soliciting teacher input. This not only diminishes morale but also falls short of grasping a full understanding of needs and contextual characteristics. While administrative meetings and decision making are ultimately necessary, deliberate steps should be taken to gain insight from the teaching faculty. School administrators will be very aware of needs and goals that should be considered in program development, but no meeting or committee can accomplish what a well-crafted faculty survey can do in terms of gaining insight into the state of the school.

In this case, we are interested in gauging two things:

1. Teachers' level of knowledge with regard to digital literacies

2. The degree to which digital literacies are being incorporated (with the correct approach, I might add) into classroom instruction

Creating the Survey

Figure 3.1 is a sample needs assessment survey that can be used for a digital literacies professional development program. The survey includes items that are drawn from each of the digital literacies listed in Table 3.1. These items describe instructional strategies and learning environments that incorporate digital literacies and make use of relevant information and communication technologies. The survey invites each teacher participant to reflect upon his or her own teaching practices and provides three consistent response options.

Instead of grouping the items by their associated digital literacies, randomizing the questions serves to ensure the integrity of the survey. Counterexamples are also used for the same purpose. Not only do they discourage participants from rapidly selecting the affirmative response for every item, they also reveal dispositions toward certain ideas or technologies, such as the attitude that Wikipedia should be blacklisted or that social media inherently leads to the breach of student privacy.

Most importantly, be brief and keep the survey response time at 5 minutes or less. Response rates decrease drastically as the time demand increases beyond 5 or 10 minutes.

Even in the most desolate situations, there will likely be pockets of innovation that can only be pinpointed through an intentional probe. Among other things, the survey will highlight potential teacher leaders who will become essential resources in supporting the infusion of digital literacies into teaching and learning. Additionally,

Figure 3.1   Sample Classroom Instruction Survey for Teachers

Your thoughtful responses to this survey will be used to design professional development that you will find to be both purposeful and fulfilling. Thank you for your time!

A S N   (A = Almost Always, S = Sometimes, N = Never)

❏ ❏ ❏   Students employ deliberate search strategies when performing online research.
❏ ❏ ❏   Classes maintain blogs where students regularly contribute posts and comments.
❏ ❏ ❏   Working together outside of class is viewed as cheating.
❏ ❏ ❏   E-portfolios are an integrated part of the class curriculum.
❏ ❏ ❏   Students are banned from using Wikipedia as a source for research and writing.
❏ ❏ ❏   The teacher empowers students to take charge of their own learning.
❏ ❏ ❏   Students use social bookmarking lists to organize exemplary websites using tags.
❏ ❏ ❏   The teacher models online reading comprehension strategies for students.
❏ ❏ ❏   Technology is used mainly by the teacher and to a lesser extent by students.
❏ ❏ ❏   The teacher encourages students to use online research databases.
❏ ❏ ❏   Google is the first stop when students look for something on the Internet.
❏ ❏ ❏   The teacher maintains a blog and is the sole contributor.
❏ ❏ ❏   Students develop e-portfolios that follow them throughout their school career.
❏ ❏ ❏   Technology is used by students to facilitate collaborative learning activities.
❏ ❏ ❏   Instructional activities involve students creating and publishing online content.
❏ ❏ ❏   Social networking is blacklisted as it relates to school and learning.
❏ ❏ ❏   A variety of web-based tools are used by students to facilitate higher order thinking.
❏ ❏ ❏   Instructional strategies stay the same when new technology is introduced.
❏ ❏ ❏   Students are challenged to contribute to the collective intelligence of online networks.
❏ ❏ ❏   Writing involves intentional collaboration among students.
❏ ❏ ❏   The majority of class time involves students focusing their attention on the teacher.
❏ ❏ ❏   Students contribute research-based information to relevant topics on Wikipedia.
❏ ❏ ❏   Mobile devices are not allowed in the classroom.
❏ ❏ ❏   Collaborative document platforms are used for peer editing and coauthoring papers.
❏ ❏ ❏   The teacher incorporates the rules of netiquette into content-focused learning activities.
❏ ❏ ❏   Student privacy is seen as a reason to avoid online social networks.
❏ ❏ ❏   Most classes are spent with students collaborating to accomplish learning objectives.
❏ ❏ ❏   Mobile devices are used to enable situated learning and instant collaboration.
❏ ❏ ❏   Students learn how to safely manage an online identity across the Internet.
❏ ❏ ❏   Students develop information literacy skills by curating topics of interest.
❏ ❏ ❏   Students write fanfiction and/or create derivative products from open content.
❏ ❏ ❏   Efforts are made to bridge the digital divide through creative instructional strategies.
❏ ❏ ❏   The teacher disseminates information to students and parents through social media.
❏ ❏ ❏   Assessment is authentic and involves real-world applications of knowledge and skills.
❏ ❏ ❏   Students combine data from multiple sources in order to convey new meaning.
❏ ❏ ❏   The teacher discourages the use of online resources due to concerns of validity.
❏ ❏ ❏   Self- and peer-assessment are regular elements in the class.
❏ ❏ ❏   Digital communication between teacher and student is considered inappropriate.
❏ ❏ ❏   Students are provided multiple options for accomplishing learning objectives.
❏ ❏ ❏   Projects are published online in order to contribute to the collective intelligence.

survey responses can be analyzed to determine the specific areas that need particular emphasis, which should guide the development of a contextualized list of digital literacies and a plan for implementing them through professional development. An online version of this needs assessment, as well as a guide for interpreting and scoring the results, can be found on this book's companion website at http://www.digitalliteracies.net.

Timing Is Key

When executing the teacher survey, it is important to consider how to best facilitate the process. It seems that in today's busy world, allowing an extended period of time to complete a task is not necessarily effective in terms of response rates. A number of studies suggest that Monday afternoon is a good time to release a survey invitation with a deadline of Thursday of the following week. Fridays, weekends, and Monday mornings are time periods commonly spent hastily flushing e-mail in-boxes. Send multiple reminders. Evidence shows that most respondents complete surveys within 24 hours of receiving the request. Otherwise, the message gets either deleted or lost in a long list of e-mails. Table 3.2 presents an ideal schedule for conducting a needs assessment survey.

Of course, there is always a group that will not participate regardless of how many times it is prompted. Below are some of the most commonly cited reasons for not responding to a survey:

- Lack of time
- Technical difficulties

Table 3.2   Schedule for Conducting a Needs Assessment Survey

Day	Action
Monday (afternoon)	Mass e-mail with survey invitation
	Paper-and-pencil version of survey by mail or other
Thursday	E-mail reminder and thank-you messages (personalized)
Monday	E-mail reminder (personalized)
	Second copy of paper-and-pencil survey by mail or other
Thursday	E-mail thank-you messages (personalized)
	Poll nonrespondents for feedback

- Survey length
- Low interest
- Concerns of how data will be used
- The complexity of survey questions

When planning a survey, consider how each of these conditions might be addressed. One way of countering those who may not see value in the effort is to include a positive, motivating statement at the beginning of the survey, which establishes a clear purpose and communicates how the responses will be used. Notice the opening statement used in the sample needs assessment survey in Figure 3.1.

Delivery Method

There are several powerful web tools that can really enhance survey results while simplifying the process. SurveyMonkey is a popular platform that offers a free option in addition to tiered paid plans. Qualtrics is a powerful platform that is popular among universities and corporations alike. Google Docs offers multifaceted survey functionality through the web form features that are integrated into its spreadsheet tool. One advantage of the Google tool is that it integrates seamlessly with its other apps. Google Apps is a constantly growing set of information and communication tools that are both free and web based. They counter the potential for data and process fragmentation in projects by bringing tools together under a common umbrella. Users need only to maintain one log-in account and are able to facilitate privacy, sharing, and collaboration with a great level of control.

While web-based surveys are definitely the way to go, it is still essential to offer multiple options. Providing a paper-and-pencil version of the survey may require extra time and expense, but it will render additional responses from those individuals who may encounter technology issues or who simply prefer that format. Indeed, it may seem counterproductive to employ a paper-and-pencil format as part of a digital literacies program; however, at this point the goal is to encourage all stakeholders to participate in the survey.

A Modular Approach

There are a variety of professional development formats or models that can be used as modular pieces of a comprehensive program. The advantage of a modular approach is the ability to select and use the components that are most appropriate in each unique context while also capitalizing on the strengths of each one. Indeed, the program is strongest and most effective with all parts intact, but each piece can stand alone or be recombined with another if necessary. Furthermore, an ancillary purpose for adopting a modular approach here is to make program adaptation as easy as possible across a wide range of target environments.

Program leaders may choose to include survey items in the needs assessment in order to gather information regarding teachers' preferred professional development formats. However, the degree to which these preferences can be accommodated may be largely influenced by the availability of time and personnel. Chapter 2 presented both traditional and innovative approaches to professional development that can be incorporated into a digital literacies initiative. Several of those modalities are described here in context, serving unique purposes and at the same time complementing each other. They include faculty seminars, PLCs, peer mentoring, and self-directed activities.

> **A modular approach provides the ability to select the most appropriate components and capitalize on the strengths of each one.**

Faculty Seminars

One of the most common formats—which will serve as a good place to start—is the faculty seminar. If an initial program is implemented over the span of one school year, then ideally each month should focus on a single aspect of digital literacies—each building on those introduced previously. During the first week of the month, the faculty meets together in a full group session where a new aspect of digital literacies is introduced in a presentation format that leverages teacher participation. This is not the time to roll a dull slideshow. Instead, this is a valuable opportunity to model authentic instructional integration of digital literacies. This does not necessarily require an extended meeting. Much can be accomplished in an hour, although extended time or additional sessions may serve to drive it home more so than a 45-minute after-school meeting might effectively accomplish.

It is important to think of the teachers as learners who need well-executed instruction that is differentiated in order to meet their unique learning styles and preferences. The last thing teachers need in a late-afternoon meeting after a taxing day is a sit-and-get presentation in a dimly lit room. Furthermore, a significant percentage of teachers are digital immigrants. Many still perceive technology as foreign and unnatural. Others fall short of finding value in virtual communities. Still some are eager to move forward but need a hand to hold along the way.

Each faculty seminar should be led by someone who is skilled in teaching and learning with digital literacies. Faculty members may buy in more eagerly when professional development is facilitated by teacher leaders as opposed to administrators or outside consultants. This may potentially be a different person for each faculty seminar, or it may be a team of leaders. Chapter 4 addresses leadership and support systems in depth.

Adult learning theory tells us that mature learners desire to know the purpose of instructional activities in order to fully engage, both cognitively and emotionally. Once clear objectives have been communicated, the session facilitator can proceed with defining the specific digital literacies in focus and present authentic examples of classroom instruction and instances of use out in the real world. It is at this time when teacher learners should be actively engaged in collaborative learning, much as it would happen in a classroom.

Consider the following example of a digital literacies presentation to kick off a month-long focus:

Example: Jason led a large-group presentation on using mobile devices to facilitate information retrieval and collaboration. This emphasis was tied into the Common Core Standards where they address the use of appropriate technology and the Internet to locate information efficiently as well as to interact and collaborate with others. He asked faculty members to bring their mobile phones to the session—making his request early and issuing multiple reminders via e-mail, mailroom flyers, and intercom announcements. As participants entered the training room, they were instructed by signage to pick up an informational handout containing mobile learning strategies and resources and a separate slip with instructions for *bell-ringer* or *as-you-enter* tasks to perform in the moments prior to the beginning of the presentation. This not only added to the instructional time, but also served to grab the attention of the participants so that they might begin focusing in on the session content and reduce or eliminate wasted time. Box 3.1 lists the pre-session tasks included on the slip of paper.

Box 3.1

"As You Enter" Slip

1. Take Handout: "Mobile Learning Strategies & Resources"
2. Download QR Reader (see bottom of handout)
3. Scan QR Code to access mobile learning wiki page
4. Begin reading information on wiki page and on handout
5. Use your phone to send a TEXT MESSAGE containing KEY CHARACTERISTICS or IDEAS of mobile learning to [my Google Voice number] (*see Chapters 2 & 7 regarding tech tools)

By the time the session started, teachers had already gained a basic familiarity with the concept of information retrieval and collaboration as enabled by mobile technology. The leader had not yet spoken a single word! (Not everyone had a smartphone, and although all faculty members owned phones with texting capability, a few individuals did not make it to the meeting with their phone in hand. Certainly, 1:1 technology is not a reality in most cases, but don't let that scare you away from employing digital literacies skills in your instructional activities because there is always a way to facilitate *one-to-some* technology arrangements.) Rather than using a PowerPoint presentation to share static information, the presenter preloaded a series of websites that allowed him to easily click from site to site in a linear fashion and demonstrate a variety of mobile learning tools and strategies using authentic activities that involved the teachers participating with their mobile phones. They were experiencing instructional activities that they could immediately apply in their own content-area lessons with very little modification. They performed research on the fly with the slew of tools available within Google Mobile. The leader solicited learner feedback using PollEverywhere.com and facilitated a brainstorming session using a digital bulletin board he created at Wiffiti.com. He sent a group text message in under 30 seconds with the Beluga app and demonstrated the idea of a mobile scavenger hunt as a learning activity with the SCVNGR app. Finally, Jason incorporated an assessment piece by asking teachers to call in to his Google Voice number and record a brief message sharing how they might use mobile learning strategies in their own classes. (This last activity demonstrates how even the most basic mobile phones can be used productively in instructional activities.)

The initial presentation is a sort of launch party for each new digital literacies focus. As was established in Chapter 2, marketing plays a key role in determining the degree of success or failure of a professional development initiative. The attitudes and efforts of teachers as they collaborate in their PLCs and work in their classrooms can be impacted significantly by the approach that is taken during the faculty seminar.

Professional Learning Communities

It is important that PLCs follow up together within a week after the initial large-group presentation. Because curriculum development is unique for each content area, homogenous grouping can prove to be beneficial when PLCs are being used for this purpose. In other cases—such as when there is an emphasis on horizontal collaboration—PLCs can function more effectively with heterogeneous membership.

The very first task of the PLCs at the beginning of a digital literacies professional development program is to establish a platform by which they will experiment, apply, and reflect.

A wiki is an excellent option for this. A wiki is a web space that allows multiple contributors to post and edit content using tools that are similar to those found in common word processing applications. A few examples of wiki platforms include Google Sites, Wikispaces, and PBwiki. While some programs may opt for all PLCs to collaborate on a single wiki, there are many advantages to allowing each individual PLC to create and maintain their own wiki. First of all, it gives teachers more ownership in their efforts. Furthermore, it allows them the experience of working with the tool in an uninhibited environment.

> **The first PLC task in the digital literacies program is establishing an online platform by which to experiment, apply, and reflect.**

While there are a variety of other platforms that can be used for organizing teachers' digital literacies efforts—such as private social networks—we will move forward here with the wiki as our platform of choice. Each and every subsequent digital literacies tool and skill will build upon this initial wiki platform, so it is essential that the platform be established as a first step at the initial launch of the program.

Experimenting: Play Is Okay

Sometimes playing with something is the best way to learn how to use it. This is especially true when dealing with technology! Teachers need—and want—a designated space and time to experiment with the tools and strategies they are being asked to implement within their classroom instruction. In fact, teachers should be *encouraged* to experiment—and innovate! The wiki is perfect for this. Teachers can create unlimited pages and later delete them if they choose. Figure 3.2 shows a screenshot of a PLC wiki where each teacher has logged an example of a learning activity he or she has implemented that incorporates digital literacies. The screenshot in Figure 3.3 shows where teachers in a PLC have posted student project artifacts from digital literacies-infused learning experiences. Finally, Figure 3.4 provides an example of a wiki that is being used both for the PLC and for communication with students and parents.

The surprisingly familiar, user-friendly editing interface removes the middleman and allows each person to work hands-on without the need for extensive training. Each PLC can choose to make its wiki public or keep it private, but it should be at least made available for access by the full faculty for the benefit of sharing and collaboration.

The Common Core State Standards address the importance of seamlessly integrating technology with nondigital forms of communication and information management. The wiki provides a medium by which both students and teachers alike can accomplish that, with an extremely high level of relevancy.

Beyond initially setting up the wikis, the purpose of PLCs in a digital literacies professional development program is to serve as a forum for making actual connections between the digital literacies and classroom instruction. These content-specific groupings provide an excellent environment for teachers to brainstorm, research, and plan how they will incorporate the digital literacies into their respective

Figure 3.2   Screenshot of Wiki Page: Teachers Reflecting Upon Instruction

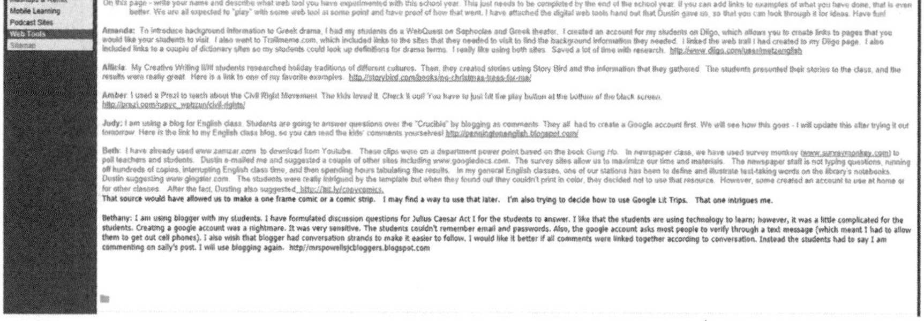

Source: Russellville High School, Russellville, Arkansas, 2010–2011 school year

Figure 3.3   Screenshot of Teacher's Site: Student Learning Artifacts

Source: Russellville High School, Russellville, Arkansas, 2010–2011 school year

Figure 3.4   Screenshot of Wiki: Digital Literacies Emphasis Incorporating Elements for Teachers, Students, and Parents

Source: Russellville High School, Russellville, Arkansas, 2010–2011 school year

courses. Each person has unique strengths that can be contributed to the overall efforts of the PLC in order to magnify the impact of the digital literacies emphasis.

Collective Knowledge

In addition to providing a place to experiment with new tools and strategies, the PLC's wiki also serves as an e-portfolio where teachers post lesson plans, activity descriptions, and student learning artifacts related to each digital literacies emphasis. Over the course of the program implementation, PLCs engage in *curation* as they collect and organize original and shared ideas and materials. The wiki provides evidence to measure program results and support assertions regarding short- and long-term impacts on teaching and learning. When maintained in an ongoing fashion throughout the initiative, the wiki as an e-portfolio allows PLCs to have instant share-out sessions as a full faculty where they discuss their efforts thus far as a sort of formative evaluation. These share-out sessions should occur near the end of each semester at minimum. In addition to serving as a benchmark and keeping teachers accountable within the program, sharing sessions are highly motivating and strengthen morale among the faculty as a whole. It is inspiring to learn firsthand about the efforts and successes of peers and colleagues.

Reflecting

While the wiki does provide a means by which teachers can reflect upon their teaching as they post artifacts, review peer contributions, and make annotations, some PLCs may also choose to start a blog where they can adopt a journal-like format to share ideas and reflect on attempts at new learning activities. Of course, the blog can be connected to the PLC's wiki in order that everything might be integrated together. A sample blog entry might read like this:

> I decided to have my students create digital posters about music careers. I provided them with links to a few potential web tools, such as Glogster and Wix. Those two seemed to work the best. Some of the others either weren't intuitive, ran slow on the school network, or turned out to be inadvertently blocked by the school content filter. I have talked to the technology director, and he has agreed to unblock that particular website since there is nothing objectionable about it. This project is going quicker than I thought because most of my students are so fluent with the technology. Their projects are very impressive! Has anyone else tried digital posters instead of collages or banners in the hallway? Any suggestions?

Pursuing Results

The PLC is an essential component in a successful digital literacies professional development program. It enables collaboration and sharing that would otherwise be less likely to occur in a large-group, meet-and-disperse approach. It also provides a means by which other nonrelated business—for instance, calendar alignment or event planning—can be taken care of without scheduling an additional meeting.

While the monthly full-faculty seminar is appropriate for disseminating knowledge and modeling strategies, the subsequent PLC meeting allows for brainstorming and experimentation, planning for instructional integration, collaboration, and reflection.

Peer Mentoring

As mentioned before, the beauty of this approach to professional development is the way in which it draws from a variety of models and formats in order to leverage the best of each. Peer mentoring can be used either formally or informally within the digital literacies program as a way to provide additional strength to the individual support system.

While peer mentors may naturally emerge from within each PLC, it is worthwhile to take time to expressly pair teachers either within or across content areas. For example, place geometry teachers together so they can focus on their common subject. Pair a newer teacher with a more experienced teacher, and encourage the more senior teacher to invite new ideas and approaches from the fresh perspective of the novice. Provide sample mentoring strategies, activities, and resources to encourage productivity and ongoing functionality among the peer mentors. Ask for informal reflections at predetermined intervals (e.g., at the end of each grading quarter) in order to gauge how the mentoring effort is progressing. Based on those reflections and other feedback, determine the appropriate point in time for re-pairing mentors—whether it be at the end of the year, sooner, or later. Constantly strive to embed peer mentoring into the overall professional development program and avoid creating additional tasks or expectations that seem disconnected. A deliberate, well-planned approach always tends to render more desired results compared to one that allows things to fall together as they may.

Peer mentors can observe each other facilitating learning activities that involve the digital literacies. The observing teacher might take that opportunity to video record the lesson so that the teacher being observed can review the lesson and engage in reflection for the purpose of instructional improvement.

Peer mentors in a PLC can team up and try new learning activities across multiple classes, engaging in a sort of modified coteaching. Consider this example:

> *Example:* Jackie and Andrea are team teachers. Since their classes are reading the same works of literature, they decide to set up a blog where their students will post entries at regular intervals in response to reflective prompts. They enable the comment feature on the blog and direct their students to respond to at least three other blog posts for each iteration of the activity. The blog provides a medium for reflection at the upper levels of Bloom's Taxonomy and enlarges the learning environment beyond the four walls of the classroom. It does not replace classroom discussion but instead augments it. By working together, Jackie and Andrea were able to share observations from multiple perspectives and strengthen the activity beyond what could have been done alone.

Assessment

If administrators decide to implement assessment pieces into the digital literacies program, peer mentoring is often the appropriate level at which to do it. Reflections, rubrics, checklists, and inventories are assessment tools that can be used by peer mentors to improve teaching. Teachers may find it less threatening when their peers are involved in facilitating assessments as opposed to administrators. In any case, administrators should clarify whether observations and evaluations are formal in nature with a direct connection to annual reviews, whether data will be analyzed for broad decision making related to school-wide instructional improvement, or if their purpose is solely for personal feedback and reflection. Many questions and misperceptions can be averted by establishing these criteria up front.

Self-Study

Each layer of teacher grouping in the digital literacies professional development program nests together to provide a healthy amount of redundancy and an efficient support system. Peer mentors are paired within each PLC, and each PLC is a homogeneous grouping formed from the faculty at large. Still, each individual teacher is responsible for his or her own professional growth. This includes a reasonable amount of self-study.

Self-study may take the form of a book review, additional college work, a noncredit course, independent travel to a professional conference, curriculum revision, or the development of a personal learning network. This is an important piece in terms of locking in the long-term impact.

School leaders should cultivate a culture among their faculty where self-initiated professional development is widespread and commonplace—and not merely another expectation. Leaders can begin by setting a positive example and engaging in their own self-directed professional development activities. Teachers, however, are often unaware that this is already happening. To solve that predicament, an administrator might consider maintaining a blog where he or she reflects and shares relevant information with faculty, students, and parents. Teachers should be provided with guidelines that outline various types of self-study and denote the criteria for earning official professional development credit for such activities. In addition to contributing to required annual hours, school systems may choose to incentivize faculty self-study through methods such as the following:

- Additional release time
- Public recognition
- In-house credentials
- Salary scale advancements
- Stipends

Chapter 5 expands upon motivation, marketing, and incentives as they relate to professional development.

Personal Learning Networks

A fresh approach to lifelong learning that combines self-study with peer mentoring and PLCs is the personal learning network (PLN). It falls under the category of self-study simply because it is initiated and facilitated by the individual. However, it capitalizes on the vast potential of online collaboration through virtual communities and web-enabled communication modalities.

The rise in popularity of the PLN is due largely to the growth of diverse social media platforms and discipline-specific social networks.

RSS readers such as Feedly allow users to subscribe to blogs and read, organize, and share updates from all of the blogs in one convenient location. (RSS stands for Really Simple Syndication.) Facebook allows users to friend other users, like pages and groups created by businesses and organizations, and follow their updates in a news feed. Twitter allows users to follow other users' tweets and set up topic-specific lists. Google+ is a social network that allows users to create circles and place other users in those circles in order to control sharing and privacy. Posts from users are displayed in each circle's stream (similar to Facebook's news feed). Ning and Edmodo are platforms that allow users to actually create their own social networks and manage all aspects including users, membership, content, features, and much more. Classroom 2.0 is an example of a custom social network created especially for educators who are interested in employing interactive web tools and social media within their instructional practices.

> **A PLN is about both *gathering* new knowledge and also *supporting* the professional growth of other educators around the world.**

Social networks have gotten a bad rap for being a place where people post pointless and self-serving status updates about their life. However, there are indeed a multitude of creative individuals who have harnessed the potential of these communication tools both productively and efficiently within a professional context. The point of a PLN is to leverage the power of all of these information sources as they relate to a particular discipline, which could be as specific as Shakespearian literature or as broad as educational leadership.

The best way to start developing a PLN is to locate two or three interesting blogs and subscribe to them. A feed reader is really the way to go as opposed to subscribing by e-mail or revisiting each blog's website regularly. A feed reader is an application that displays the content from multiple blogs or websites together on one clean, organized screen—similar to how an e-mail application such as Microsoft Outlook allows a user to manage multiple e-mail addresses in one place.

The key to a successful experience with a PLN is focusing in on a few outstanding resources and then consuming the information without *becoming* consumed by spending hours wading through a flood of social media feeds. In this case, less is more. Also keep in mind that the unsubscribe button is always just a click away! A PLN is a living, breathing community that constantly grows and shrinks as new, better resources are discovered and potentially take the place of existing content sources.

Beyond blogs, Twitter is a great place to get bite-sized morsels of inspiration and new ideas for innovative curriculum and instruction. An aggregator such as TweetDeck or HootSuite makes it extremely easy to follow topics and organize feeds on both Facebook and Twitter. Aggregators are applications that can be downloaded for free onto computers and smartphones. Many aggregators also have web browser-based interfaces that enable access when users are away from their primary computer. Paper.li is another web-based tool that makes Twitter content more manageable by automatically publishing a daily or weekly online newspaper containing the most relevant and popular tweets on a given topic.

Google+ is a rapidly growing social network that conveniently integrates Google's expansive suite of apps in addition to a progressive set of social media features. Scoop.it allows users to become curators of web content by creating online magazines that can be easily shared.

All of these platforms offer potential sources of knowledge that can become part of a teacher's PLN. However, establishing a PLN is only the first step. Active participation is necessary in order to truly reap the full benefits. It requires not only consuming content but also making regular contributions to the collective intelligence that is afforded by the Internet and social media. Consider these suggestions for making a meaningful contribution:

- Maintain a blog for reflecting and sharing new ideas.
- Spread the word about the blog through Google+ and Twitter.
- Ask thought-provoking questions at the end of blog posts to encourage readers to comment.
- Use Twitter to share gems of 140 characters or less and retweet posts from other users.

Over time, a base of followers will develop who are seeking out resources for their own PLNs. It is exciting to realize that a PLN is not just about gathering personal knowledge but is also about supporting the professional growth of other educators around the world.

These are just a few suggestions for getting started with a PLN. Try to set aside one or more time slots on a weekly basis to participate in a PLN. In some cases, it may be appropriate to schedule time daily, but in general, two or three times per week will put most people on the verge of information overload. Again, keep everything within moderation.

Table 3.3 outlines a sample PLN and describes the relationship between social media tools, professional networking, information consumption, and purposeful contribution by the teacher.

Table 3.3   Example of a Music Teacher's Personal Learning Network

Social Media	Networking	Consuming	Contributing
Blogs	• Post comments on other blogs in order to engage constructive dialogue with authors and other readers. • Periodically invite guest authors (colleagues, students, and outside experts) to contribute. • Occasionally assist other teachers with their blogs.	• Subscribed to a few select blogs (mustech.net, etc.) and typically read new posts twice weekly (using Feedly). • Use annotation tools to mark up and save key ideas for future research and teaching, etc.	• Maintain a blog on Blogger and write weekly posts with new ideas, resources, reflections, and research. • Blog is configured to automatically post an announcement and link on Twitter and Google+ to catch those readers who are not directly subscribed to the blog.
Diigo	• Created a social bookmarking group where multiple people can collect links to high-quality websites that contain ideas, resources, and research for teaching music.	• Begin web searches by searching Diigo for links saved by other users before searching the open Internet. • Follow users who tend to contribute valuable resources regularly.	• Bookmark valuable websites, make those links public, and attach tags to make searching easier for others. • New links are automatically shared via Twitter; latest bookmarks are displayed in a widget on my blog.
Twitter	• Retweet others' posts that are particularly meaningful, and reply to posts to engage dialogue. • Participate in #musedchat where music educators chat live weekly via Twitter about a specific topic established on-the-fly.	• Use TweetDeck to automatically search and display tweets related to topics in upcoming lessons. • Subscribe to a couple of Paper.li e-news papers to receive digests of top Twitter content.	• Post quick ideas on-the-go, links to new resources, and more using mobile apps. • Automatically publish a daily e-newspaper using Paper.li that contains recent tweets related to music and specific topics I am currently focusing on.

Table 3.3   Continued

Social Media	Networking	Consuming	Contributing
Google+	• Created a Music PLN circle and added fellow music teachers, state composers, and guest conductors in order to exchange ideas and collaborate on projects.	• Created streams for iPad music apps, wind band literature, and innovative marching band techniques that displays related posts being contributed across Google+.	• Post key thoughts and ideas gleaned from books I read, workshops, conferences, the classroom, and other professional activities.
YouTube SchoolTube TeacherTube	• Follow certain channels (including BerkleeMusic) that produce high-quality content. Post comments and send messages to the creators.	• Locate videos and create playlists based upon topics (e.g., history, theory, performances).	• Create *teachlet* videos for class and post online; use sharing links to share newly posted videos via my blog, Twitter, and Google+.

Individual Classroom Integration

PLCs in their fullest sense exist as more than a monthly meeting. As they mature, teachers find themselves engaged in ongoing, informal communication throughout the month. Goals are set—not only at the school or district level but also within PLCs—for applying each of the digital literacies within classroom instruction. This will certainly be different for each institution, but a reasonable goal might be for every teacher to experiment, hands-on, with each month's digital literacies focus and each PLC as a whole to implement at least one digital literacies-infused instructional segment per month. Even though it might not be realistic to expect every teacher in every PLC to achieve a *full* implementation within a limited time frame, all PLC members should be involved in planning, applying, reflecting, sharing, and documenting. If this approach is adopted, then by the end of the year, every teacher will have experienced a legitimate degree of teaching and learning with digital literacies. Indeed, the groundwork will be laid for further curriculum development and instructional improvement.

Individual Consultations and Training and Support Resources

The importance of training and support when dealing with technology cannot be overemphasized. Because contracting outside experts and hiring additional personnel are typically not feasible options, a train-the-trainer approach is highly recommended—where skilled leaders are equipped through training that occurs outside of and prior to the main series of professional development activities. For example, a technology leader might be trained and placed in each PLC. This person provides much-needed direction and support related to the digital literacies efforts while the PLC chairperson provides general leadership to the group. A train-the-trainer approach might also be used when delegates are sent to a conference and return with new knowledge and skills that are to be disseminated by other individuals through the faculty seminars.

It is important to mention here that teacher leaders should be made available for working individually with those who need and desire one-on-one assistance with instructional technology and curriculum development as they relate to digital literacies. A wiki can also be developed as a support site where resources are posted and the use of digital literacies is modeled for teachers. All of this and more will be discussed at length in Chapter 4, which addresses leadership roles and support structures.

Program Time Line

The time line for implementation will determine the extent to which the elements described in this chapter can be incorporated into a school's program. A broad time line for the first semester might look similar to the sample schedule shown in Table 3.4.

Consider using a monthly cycle. Its relatively short span allows for frequent contact and benchmarking as opposed to going weeks without any follow-up. Faculty seminars and PLC meetings might be held on Wednesdays after school for an hour, with faculty seminars on the first week and PLC meetings on the second and fourth weeks of the month. Peer mentors can collaborate during their prep periods, at lunch, before and after school, or asynchronously via various communication modalities. If full days are available for professional development, those can be used for PLC share-out sessions and intensive training opportunities. Above all, make it a point to allow teachers ample time for planning, development, and collaboration.

Table 3.4 Sample Program Implementation Schedule

May–July	Administrative planning including needs assessment for upcoming school year
August	6 hours of pre-school PD designated for digital literacies program kickoff (formats: faculty seminar and PLC)
September	Faculty seminar: Introduce one or more digital literacies
	PLC meetings: Plan for instructional integration
	Ongoing peer mentoring and self-study
	Individual planning, instruction, and reflection
October	Similar to September
November	Similar to September and October
December	Midpoint survey (formative assessment)
	PLC share-out day
	Review feedback and modify as needed for upcoming semester

Program Evaluation

Too many professional development initiatives are set in motion with a gung ho approach, only to be abandoned at the conclusion (if not earlier) for something new—with no look at results or impact. Did the efforts of leaders and participants bring forth fruit? There may be no way of knowing, if time is not taken to collect data and analyze change. Data collection should be performed at multiple levels.

Session Evaluations

First of all, develop a generic participant evaluation form—such as the one shown in Figure 3.5—that can be completed quickly and used for any type of event, whether it is a full-faculty seminar or a miniconference breakout session. Include both open response and Likert-scale questions. Keep the evaluation anonymous in order to encourage open and honest feedback. Ask participants in each and every formal session to complete an evaluation form and submit it before leaving the room. Allow a minute or two for this prior to the conclusion of the session so that participants do not feel that they are using their own personal time to complete the task. In addition to using paper evaluations, a variety of mobile apps and web tools can be leveraged for the purpose of garnering participant feedback.

Figure 3.5   Session Evaluation Form

What are some of the strengths of this session?
What are some of the weaknesses of this session?
Please rate the format and delivery of this session: Poor 1   2   3   4   5   Excellent
Please rate the usefulness of the information shared: Not At All 1   2   3   4   5 Extremely
What topics would you suggest for future sessions?

This next step is critical! Review the results immediately follow-ing the session, and identify any changes that need to be made to future efforts. Everyone has a tendency to say they will look at some-thing later and then end up getting busy with other things and never look back. Evaluation data is only useful if it is used! Many times management experts advise that mail should be handled only twice: once when it is initially opened and reviewed and a second and final time when action is taken to deal with the tasks presented by the mail's contents. Perhaps this approach might also be applied to pro-gram evaluation data. Keep in mind that the purpose of formative evaluation is to make program improvements midstream in order that an *immediate* impact might be seen.

Midpoint and End-of-Year Surveys

Individual session evaluations provide instant feedback and allow for rapid improvements to be made to training and support programs. However, these evaluation instruments can only begin to skim the surface. Indeed, they must be short and simple enough to compel participants to complete them, even as frequently as every time a formal session is held.

A more in-depth and lengthy survey is appropriate at a program's midpoint—perhaps at the end of the fall semester—and at the end of the school year when a program either culminates or rolls over into a second year. This evaluation can serve to gain insight into which digital literacies and technology tools need reemphasis. Furthermore, it can help to identify emerging teacher leaders.

When rolling over into a second-year program, this survey gar-ners much-needed data for planning and refocusing based upon the changing needs of the faculty, students, and curriculum. As always, it cannot be overemphasized how important it is to provide rationale for all of these surveys. Evidence shows that participant buy-in greatly increases when this detail is addressed expressly.

PLC Share-Out Days

Finding time to share and reflect can be difficult amidst tight schedules and packed agendas. However, one of the key elements of this program is sharing and collaboration, and it needs to happen at all levels. PLC Share-Out Days bring the entire faculty together. Each PLC shares about their digital literacies activities and uses their wiki/e-portfolio to show artifacts from instructional activities. Presentations need not necessarily be formal. An entire session with multiple PLCs presenting might be a short as an hour or last much longer, depending on the number of PLCs and the available time frame. PLC Share-Out Days should be scheduled at least once per semester and more often if appropriate.

Building on the Best

Effective professional development is not solely invested in one particular doctrine. Instead, it draws upon the best of multiple approaches in order to accomplish the goals established after performing the needs assessment. Faculty seminars, PLCs, peer mentoring, and self-study go hand in hand to support the integration of digital literacies all the way from the top-level professional development activities and ultimately into each teacher's curriculum and instruction.

Emerging Leaders

Teacher leaders play a key role in the unique results achieved through the approach described in this book for planning and implementing a digital literacies professional development program. Correctly identifying and preparing the right faculty members to perform leadership functions will have a significant impact on the success of the overall program as well as each person involved. Additionally, certain nonhuman support structures should be established and maintained as essential elements for meeting the needs of all program stakeholders. This and more is addressed in the next chapter.

QUESTIONS FOR REFLECTION AND DISCUSSION

1. How might this approach to digital literacies professional development build upon some of the basic training and support structures that are already in place within the school?

2. In terms of how teachers are currently addressing digital literacies within instruction, what needs are likely to surface through a school-wide needs assessment?

3. What might be the best approach for rolling out a comprehensive program like the one described in this chapter? Why is this the same or different compared to what might work in another school or environment?

4

Teacher Leaders and Support Structures

The importance of solid, multilevel leadership within the context of the digital literacies professional development program cannot be overstated. Such roles include leadership at the administrative level but leverage particularly widespread involvement of teacher leaders. Leadership is needed at the full-faculty level, within each PLC, and on a peer-to-peer basis. Teacher technology leaders should be identified or, if applicable, placed within each PLC in addition to the primary leadership role in order to provide adequate support to teachers as they work to develop their own digital literacies while also attempting to integrate such competencies into their classroom instruction.

Authors and speakers such as John Maxwell, Seth Godin, and Jim Collins have contributed immensely to our understanding of how effective leadership can be achieved and top-notch organizations created. Fortunately, their ideas are not limited to the corporate world. Indeed, they can be applied across all disciplines. Almost any of their books and other publications would be beneficial to your leadership and organizational development efforts. As a starting point, I might recommend *The 5 Levels of Leadership* by John Maxwell, and *Good to Great* by Jim Collins. I would also encourage you to read two of Seth Godin's thought-provoking books, *Linchpin* and *Tribes*.

Leadership development is a worthwhile investment, not only for school and district administrators but also for teacher leaders and the entire teaching faculty. Indeed, we all need to develop ourselves as leaders. Leaders are not limited to just administrators, chairs, instructional coaches, etc. In fact, everyone can—and should—be a leader through the roles they fill in their organizations. It is important to debunk the myth that leadership is only for the boss. Everyone's involved. Teachers can no longer pass the buck. If everyone steps up to the plate and takes responsibility to lead as part of the team, great things start to happen. And it is through this realization that the vital importance of leadership development comes into focus.

> Leadership development is a worthwhile investment for administrators, teacher leaders, and the entire faculty.

Leadership goes hand in hand with support. Ongoing and readily-accessible support is of utmost importance in professional and organizational development, especially when technology is involved. Several potential avenues of support exist, including teacher leaders who are available for individual consultations and an online support site containing technology tutorials and examples of instructional activities. Too often, professional development initiatives fall short when it comes to support and follow-through. The discussion contained herein should be coupled with what is given in other chapters in order to counter critical mistakes that can lead to poor results and seemingly wasted investments of time and resources.

> Professional development initiatives often fall short when it comes to support and follow-through.

Layers of Support

Tiered leadership is embedded within multiple layers of support in the digital literacies professional development program. Time and time again, testimonials from in-service teachers reaffirm what the studies show, which is that school-based educational change implementations survive or fail based largely upon the amount and quality of support and assistance that teachers receive once they are back in the classroom. This means that we cannot merely demonstrate a new instructional method in a faculty meeting, send teachers away with a one-page handout, and then expect them to successfully implement this new teaching technique in their classrooms tomorrow with total independence. This one-shot method is a surefire way to render teachers who are both demoralized and demotivated. Table 4.1 lists the different levels of support, which are essential elements of a digital literacies professional development program that aims to produce positive results and sustain lasting change.

Administrative Support and Resources

Successful change in education begins neither with a top-down nor a bottom-up approach. Instead, change begins when a positive momentum is created, resulting in systemic forward movement, and the impetus for change flows simultaneously from the bottom up and the top down. Top-down initiatives often fail to earn the buy-in of all stakeholders, while bottom-up movements tend to lack the organizational vision and leadership that lie in the hands of top-level leaders who have a better understanding of the big picture.

It is no surprise that administrative support is the first stop on the road to a successful implementation. Quite often, an initiative like the digital literacies program will be born at the administrative level, thus making this factor a nonissue. In some cases, however, the seedling effort may begin elsewhere within a school, such as within a department after several teachers have returned from an inspiring conference or workshop where they heard the results of other schools' implementations. In this situation, the teachers face the need to gain administrative buy-in. This will typically work its way up through the department and to the school-level leadership, which will then take it to curriculum directors and other district-level administrators.

Even if the push for a digital literacies professional development program is born at the administrative level, it will still be necessary to

Table 4.1 Levels of Leadership and Support

Role or Resource	Function
Administrative support and resources	Organizational backbone, personnel and finances, top-level
Program coordinator	Planning, roles, large-group training, train the trainer
Support site	Technology-based support, wiki, tutorials, samples
Individualized support	Program coordinator, PLC leaders, peers (teacher leaders)
Personal Learning Network (PLN)	On-demand, self-service support and development

gain the interest and enthusiasm of all involved administrators across the board. It is essential that they see the potential fruits of this program and understand how it fits within the larger context of professional development and curriculum and instruction. Don't make the mistake of billing it as *just another program that will fix our problems.* Digital literacies are different: revolutionary, even.

Program Coordinator

The digital literacies professional development program has the potential to be somewhat large in scope. While it does not necessitate a position dedicated solely to its leadership, it does warrant the appointment of a program coordinator. The program coordinator will work closely with administrators as he or she handles all aspects of planning and implementing the school-wide digital literacies professional development and instructional improvement initiative. The person should be a teacher leader who has the full respect of the faculty and administration and who has strong technology skills. The requirements of this position will demand some teaching release time in addition to what is already allowed for a normal teaching load. This is not only because the program coordinator will need ample time to plan and collaborate but also because he or she will be charged with providing a significant amount of individualized training and support to faculty peers.

Some schools that have sufficient resources may be able to appoint a teacher leader with complete release from teaching (i.e., no class load), while a majority of schools will likely face the need to call upon someone who can balance a lighter teaching load with this leadership role. Still others may choose to leverage coleadership by two or more teachers if it is not feasible to reduce a teaching load. In any case, teachers want to know that their leaders are *in the trenches* with them, experiencing the same day-to-day challenges and fulfilling the rigorous expectations that they are faced with. All of this serves to further leverage participant buy-in, a pivotal factor that is addressed throughout this book.

Planning

As a key planner, the program coordinator is involved in executing the needs assessment that occurs during the early stages of creating a customized digital literacies professional development program.

He or she has a good rapport with faculty school wide and is able to identify key faculty who might fill essential leadership roles within the context of the program. The program coordinator develops the organizational map, training materials, and support resources— including, but not limited to, the online support site, which is discussed shortly. This individual captures a vision for how the digital literacies professional development program fits within the context of the school as a whole and weaves it into the fabric of the school culture and the overall instructional approach. The person in this position takes the reins at overall program leadership from the very beginning. By being a middleman of sorts, the program coordinator goes a long way at fusing the relationship between faculty and administrators, thereby leveraging immense success and surpassing what is seen in other educational programs and initiatives.

Large-Group Training

Chapter 3 describes the large-group training seminars that occur on a monthly basis and at other points throughout the year. The program coordinator is responsible for either leading these or empowering other capable leaders to do so. These other leaders should come from the faculty, but on a limited basis they might be administrators or outside experts who are brought in from other schools, educational cooperatives, or training providers. Bringing in outsiders can serve to inject new ideas and perspectives that might otherwise go untapped. On the other hand, teachers also value input from colleagues who are on the frontlines with them because they can relate to the challenges they experience every day. If no one on the inside is capable of providing training on a particular topic or skill, then perhaps it might be appropriate to send one or more teachers to an outside workshop, seminar, or conference where they can gain the knowledge and skills necessary to train the faculty.

Train the Trainer

Because teacher leaders are such an important component of the digital literacies professional development program, a train-the-trainer approach can be both useful and efficient when it comes to equipping teachers with the knowledge, skills, and dispositions necessary in order to lead their colleagues. The program coordinator is responsible for planning and facilitating the train-the-trainer events. Although it might seem more logical for administrators to handle this, keep in mind that leadership within the faculty (e.g., the program coordinator) generates goodwill among teachers in a way that top-down leadership tends to fall short.

The train-the-trainer model aims to equip trainers with subject-matter expertise, instructional methods, supporting resources, and presentation or implementation skills. The training is first modeled by the program coordinator who is leading the train-the-trainer event. Then, the trainers in training should be given multiple opportunities to practice the training protocol so that they can go out and lead their colleagues with confidence.

When identifying potential trainer candidates among the faculty, program coordinators should look for teachers who fulfill many if not all of the following characteristics:

- Opinion leaders among faculty and subgroups (e.g., departments)
- Well respected by both teachers and administrators
- Not necessarily limited to tenured or seasoned faculty
- Effective at teaching, facilitating, and demonstrating
- Engaging and interesting personality (this does matter!)
- Creative *and* innovative
- Ability to build relational bridges
- Desire to learn, grow, and change
- Highly adaptable/flexible
- Cool head and warm heart
- Attitude of *we're all in this together* as opposed to *sage on the stage*

Train-the-trainer events should happen well in advance—perhaps during the summer prior to the school year when the teachers will serve as trainers. Last-minute, reactive trainings only serve to frazzle everyone involved and take away from the value of the trainer role among the faculty. Train the trainer is, indeed, a powerful model. In fact, I see it as being in line with what John Maxwell (2011) describes as Level 4 leadership where a leader is developing other leaders. This type of leadership is moving in the direction of creating sustainability within your school, which is essential if the digital literacies initiative is to last beyond the pilot year. After all, good people have a tendency of moving on to new opportunities in other organizations where they can advance their career. This is bound to happen if you place the most talented and capable leaders in positions of leadership. However, if you are constantly engaged in leadership development within your

> **Perpetual leadership development within a self-sustaining initiative means that personnel changes should not impact long-term results.**

institution and developing a digital literacies initiative that is self-sustaining, then personnel changes should not have a negative impact on your immediate and long-term program results.

Participant Leaders

Leaders should also be participants. As John Maxwell (2011, p. 136) says, be a tour guide, not a travel agent. Take people . . . don't send them. Indeed, administrators should be actively involved as peer participants in the digital literacies initiative, learning alongside everyone else. Likewise, the program coordinator should also be an active contributor to a professional learning community (PLC) and fulfill all of the requirements and expectations of the professional development activities.

When I teach a class—whether it be at the K-12 level or in higher education—I always emphasize throughout the course that I am there to learn *alongside* the students. Now, this doesn't mean that I am choosing not to fulfill my role as instructor and facilitator of learning. Instead, I am attempting to make a meaningful connection with the students and let them know that I am not above being a learner myself. It not only motivates students but also releases them to learn at a much faster pace than might otherwise be possible. Yes, I am an authority on the subject matter and a skilled teacher, but I have not somehow *arrived* at a pinnacle from which I should peer down on the learners as subordinates.

Actively participating while also leading gives leaders a window into the dynamics of how the digital literacies initiative is actually unfolding. It provides an opportunity for leaders to identify problems and address concerns that might otherwise go unnoticed or unreported. However, it is important that the program coordinator and administrators not become the ones who do everything within the PLCs, departments, and other smaller groups. It can be easy to slip into the trap of being the go-to person, particularly since he or she is the one who has played a key role in planning, training, and implementation. These leaders should learn to demonstrate a certain degree of healthy ignorance when acting as participants in teacher work groups.

Support Site

As described in Chapter 3, the framework for digital literacies professional development makes extensive use of online tools and platforms for supporting the implementation of the program and assisting faculty in their curricular modification in response to the digital literacies emphasis. If the program coordinator is the hub of human leadership and support, then the digital literacies wiki site is the technological hub of support. The program coordinator sets up the support wiki using a platform of his or her choice and maintains it on an ongoing basis. This wiki is a one-stop shop. It is an excellent location to place all kinds of instructional support materials. Indeed, the wiki is always available and within reach, whereas key support personnel will not always be accessible at each and every moment of need. But the program coordinator does not have to juggle all of this alone. He or she can invite other teachers to contribute to the wiki as they have resources and strategies to share. Wikis are highly collaborative, making them an excellent choice for an online support site. Of course, other platform types could be used quite effectively as well—for instance, those designed for highly customizable social networking—but the wiki is the platform of choice for this writing. Like so many aspects of this digital literacies professional development program, the support wiki should be a universal tool. That means in part that it is allowed to become more than a place for one person (i.e., the program coordinator) to push out resources and information to the participants.

> **If the program coordinator is the hub of human leadership and support, then the digital literacies wiki site is the technological hub of support.**

Indeed, it is yet another way to engage all teachers in collaboration and leverage complete buy-in and engagement. Teachers can be encouraged and reminded repeatedly to add to the wiki as they experience those wonderful *ah-ha* moments in their professional learning and as they come across resources they deem worthwhile to share with others. This will also help to further cultivate a community of sharing, which is so important. I am a firm believer in the exponential benefits that come from building upon a collective intelligence or a collective knowledge base. As you develop and implement your program, be ever mindful of the need to involve *everyone* in as many aspects of both the front end and the back end of this movement that is no less than a paradigm shift in the way we approach teaching and learning.

The support wiki, such as the one shown in Figure 4.1, can include the following elements:

- Schedules for trainings and other meetings
- Links to each PLC's own wikis, blogs, and other online venues
- New ideas and resources to support curricular integration

- A specific page for each of the digital literacies that includes sample lessons, learning artifacts, potential content-area applications, optional web tools, tutorials, and more
- Frequently asked questions, troubleshooting, and other help functions to help teachers resolve issues they come across during their implementation of the digital literacies
- Spotlight on teachers who are doing exemplary work in teaching with digital literacies

Individualized Support

I cannot emphasize enough the importance of putting into place solid, high-quality support systems that will be there for teachers when they are in the classroom, developing curriculum, and teaching students. This is the point that the rubber meets the road and your digital literacies initiative either soars or sinks. Support is needed at an individualized level. While it seems that we tend to invest most of our efforts into one-shot professional development attempts, the reality is that in the workforce (whether it is teaching or something totally different) we spend about 80% of our time merely surviving and learning on-the-go. Only a fraction of time is spent in formal learning experiences. This startling comparison only intensifies the need for performance support that *rides along* with teachers and is there when the need arises.

Fortunately, a well-constructed leadership plan has several layers of support in place so that no single person carries the entire load. The program coordinator works in cooperation with school

Figure 4.1   Screenshot of Support Wiki

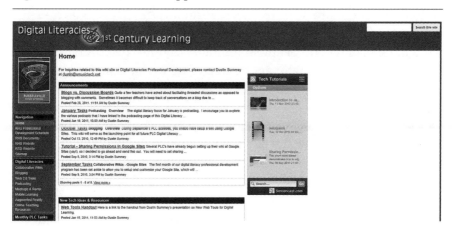

administrators to establish a tiered system of leadership that involves teachers from all parts of the faculty. PLC leaders are important points of contact who coordinate the PLC activities and facilitate collaboration among teachers. Within each PLC, a teacher who is a strong technologist serves as an instructional technology specialist and provides much-needed leadership for the PLC's digital literacies efforts throughout the process. (This is an often-overlooked intentional role within PLCs.) All of these individuals are available to provide support on a rolling basis. Still, other teacher leaders are trained to do the same so that any teacher has at least two viable options for obtaining just-in-time support, whether they are working on developing curriculum that incorporates digital literacies or perhaps in the classroom teaching students and needing assistance with a facilitation issue. Again, let's break the mind-set that only administrators are leaders. Everyone is called upon to lead through the unique role they fill within the organization. The train-the-trainer model is an excellent way to empower scores of new leaders and ramp up program effectiveness and teacher productivity.

> **A well-constructed leadership plan has several layers of support in place so that no single person carries the entire load.**

Individualized support will no doubt take on many different forms. Teachers will need assistance developing new learning activities, lesson plans, and curricular units that integrate digital literacies. This support can come through collaboration within PLCs and subject-area departments, from peer mentors, from instructional coaches, or from any other teacher leader.

Teachers will also need technical support as they work with new technology tools and use existing technologies in new ways. Lack of support in this area is a quick route to failure as many teachers will not continue to expend time and effort battling difficult technology over a long period of time without adequate and timely assistance. This is especially true of those teachers who are not digital natives. Network technicians, who are often staffed under the administrative umbrella of Information Technology, are typically not equipped with the knowledge, skills, or time to assist teachers with instructional uses of technology. Instructional coaches are not always skilled in the strategic use of technology in teaching and learning. So, it is essential to identify skilled teacher technologists and place them in each PLC while also designating them as points of contact and giving them the

> **Lack of support is a quick route to failure.**

time, resources, and flexibility necessary in order to rise to the occasion and support other teachers effectively.

This individualized support need is a place where the support wiki can really become a valuable asset to boosting the quality and success of the initiative. Tutorials, sample lesson plans, and links to online resources can be extremely useful to teachers when they are trying to make connections between ideas and actions. Teachers often tell me that they need just a little person-to-person assistance followed by some time to play with new tools and strategies on their own before following up with another round of assistance to answer questions that arise as they work on their own. Indeed, human support can never be totally replaced by technology, so the wiki should never be considered to be an alternative to a deliberate leadership plan that functions well and has some depth. Figure 4.2 shows a schematic of how the leadership support structure might fit together. This is not intended to indicate a hierarchy of any kind, but rather a relationship between leadership roles and an efficient way in which to distribute the weight of supporting an entire faculty across a number of key people. Leadership and support should be characterized more by egalitarian qualities as opposed to a complex line of reporting.

Looking for Leaders

One of the challenges of assembling a strong leadership team is—as Jim Collins (2001) puts it—getting the right people on the bus (and the wrong people off). I have reiterated the value of inclusiveness in all aspects of your program, but I must qualify that by explaining that such an approach should be highly strategic. In his book, *Good to Great*, Collins talks a lot about how the right people can enable great

Figure 4.2   Leadership and Support Structure

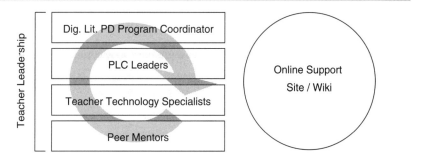

success in an organization while the wrong people can really pose a hindrance that is potentially fatal to any effort. I am not talking about slimming down your faculty by getting rid of difficult people. What I am suggesting is that the key roles in your digital literacies professional development program should be filled by the most capable people, and in this highly tiered approach to organizing your people throughout your program, those who need to be *off the bus* should find themselves at the bottom. Imagine running your personnel through a series of sieves, each slightly more selective in nature so that you can place each person at their point of best fit.

Opinion Leaders

In *The 5 Levels of Leadership*, John Maxwell states, "People buy in to the leader, *then* [emphasis added] the vision" (2011, p. 170). You can capture your faculty's buy-in by identifying those individuals who are looked upon as *opinion leaders*. These people have earned the respect of their peers and can sway the views of others in a way others simply cannot. While it is tempting to try to sell the *idea* of digital literacies to the group as a whole, it is much more effective and efficient to begin by getting your opinion leaders on board first. Being able to identify opinion leaders requires an understanding of the people, subgroups, and overall dynamics within your organization. Administrators may have an idea of who the opinion leaders are, but it is more likely that they will need to have conversations with various people throughout the school in order to truly identify who all of these opinion leaders are.

Having said all of that, it is important to recognize that good leaders do not always have buy-in from everyone. Smart leaders will acknowledge and accept that reality and discern which stakeholders to focus their attention on and how to approach the others.

The Three L's of Leadership

Leaders listen, learn, and then they lead. This is where inclusiveness can really be useful—that is, an inclusiveness of input from all stakeholders. The purpose of teacher leadership is to guide, energize, and excite participants throughout the digital literacies initiative and on the

> **Leaders listen, learn, and then they lead.**

long term. Leadership that happens concurrently from the top down and also the bottom up shows value for everyone. Good leaders encourage change as opposed to bulldogging or forcing it. Finally, someone once said, "Don't be surprised when others whine, complain, and second guess. Leaders are proven by their responses to cheap shots and challenges."

80/20 Principles

I am a big fan of 80/20 principles. I guess it's because they boil down profound realities into simple cause-and-effect relationships. Of course, the 80/20 ratio is not a scientific figure. Instead, it is a way to illustrate an input/output relationship across many contexts and disciplines. Also known as the Pareto principle, it suggests that in many situations 80% of the output comes from 20% of the input. Examining some 80/20 principles can really bring to light some important realities as you embark upon a leadership campaign. Table 4.2 lists a few 80/20 principles, several of which are mentioned in this chapter and elsewhere throughout the book. It is not a hard-and-fast list. What principles might you add?

When developing your leadership and support structure, start by identifying the top 20% of leaders in your organization. Those may fit some of the descriptors I have mentioned already in this chapter, but they will certainly become the core of your leadership support structure. Also remember that just because you can swing a hammer, it doesn't make you a carpenter. Some of the people who may have filled leadership roles in the past may not actually be good leaders. When we look at superficial details such as status, position, and precedent, we overlook essential qualities that really make a good leader. Other people make those mistakes all the time, but hopefully you are not going to do that after reading this book.

Table 4.2   80/20 Principles to Consider

80% of time is spent *surviving* and learning informally, while 20% of time is spent in formal learning.
Spend 80% of your time accomplishing the top 20% of your to-do list.
Identify the top 20% of leaders in your organization. Leverage their potential to lead the other 80%.
80% of resistance and push back will come from 20% of your faculty.
Add your 80/20 principle here: _____

Developing a Personal Learning Network (PLN)

Personal Learning Networks (PLNs) have been referenced at several points throughout this book, and Chapter 3 takes time to describe exactly how to establish a PLN. PLNs most definitely fit into the category of support structures, due to the fact that they provide a constant, on-demand stream of professional knowledge and opportunities for collaboration that can, among infinite other things, support the integration of digital literacies into teaching and learning. A PLN is professional development on demand, much like the video on demand (VOD) that we enjoy at home with digital cable or satellite television.

It would be completely appropriate to include sessions early on in the program that focus on helping teachers establish their own PLN. These sessions might explain the process of following Twitter feeds, subscribing to blogs, creating Google+ circles, and maintaining an RSS feed, for example. Teachers should be given hands-on time to explore these realms and establish their PLN during dedicated blocks of professional development, rather than merely showing a demonstration and then telling them to set up a PLN on their own time. Also, it is essential to show teachers how to grow and refine their PLN on a rolling basis so that it does not become stagnate. This concept is not too different from my fantasy football lineup. I can draft a stellar team before the season begins; but if I fail to log in frequently to manage my lineup as certain players perform poorly, become injured, or get a bye week, then my team won't do so well overall. However, if I make necessary adjustments along the way, the results tend to be much more impressive and I benefit greatly in terms of competing with the others in my fantasy league.

I am including here as Table 4.3 the sample PLN that was initially presented in Chapter 3 because I want to emphasize the importance of a PLN not only as a part of the digital literacies framework that is at the heart of this initiative but also as a key support tool that can support its overall success.

Table 4.3   Example of a Music Teacher's Personal Learning Network

Social Media	Networking	Consuming	Contributing
Blogs	• Post comments on other blogs in order to engage constructive	• Subscribed to a few select blogs (mustech.net, etc.) and typically read	• Maintain a blog on Blogger and write weekly posts with

Table 4.3   Continued

Social Media	Networking	Consuming	Contributing
	dialogue with authors and other readers. • Periodically invite guest authors (colleagues, students, and outside experts) to contribute. • Occasionally assist other teachers with their blogs.	new posts twice weekly (using Feedly). • Use annotation tools to mark up and save key ideas for future research and teaching, etc.	new ideas, resources, reflections, and research. • Blog is configured to automatically post an announcement and link on Twitter and Google+ to catch those readers who are not directly subscribed to the blog.
Diigo	• Created a social bookmarking group where multiple people can collect links to high-quality websites that contain ideas, resources, and research for teaching music.	• Begin web searches by searching Diigo for links saved by other users before searching the open Internet. • Follow users who tend to contribute valuable resources regularly.	• Bookmark valuable websites, make those links public, and attach tags to make searching easier for others. • New links are automatically shared via Twitter; latest bookmarks are displayed in a widget on my blog.
Twitter	• Retweet others' posts that are particularly meaningful, and reply to posts to engage dialogue. • Participate in #musedchat where music educators chat live weekly via Twitter about a specific topic established on-the-fly.	• Use TweetDeck to automatically search and display tweets related to topics in upcoming lessons. • Subscribe to a couple of Paper.li e-news papers to receive digests of top Twitter content.	• Post quick ideas on-the-go, links to new resources, and more using mobile apps. • Automatically publish a daily e-newspaper using Paper.li that contains recent tweets related to music and specific topics I am currently focusing on.

(Continued)

Table 4.3   Continued

Social Media	Networking	Consuming	Contributing
Google+	• Created a Music PLN circle and added fellow music teachers, state composers, and guest conductors in order to exchange ideas and collaborate on projects.	• Created streams for iPad music apps, wind band literature, and innovative marching band techniques that displays related posts being contributed across Google+.	• Post key thoughts and ideas gleaned from books I read, workshops, conferences, the classroom, and other professional activities.
YouTube SchoolTube TeacherTube	• Follow certain channels (including BerkleeMusic) that produce high-quality content. Post comments and send messages to the creators.	• Locate videos and create playlists based upon topics (e.g., history, theory, performances).	• Create teachlet videos for class and post online; use sharing links to share newly posted videos via my blog, Twitter, and Google+.

QUESTIONS FOR REFLECTION AND DISCUSSION

1. Where might the best starting point be for leadership development within the school? How does this differ from what the obvious choice might initially seem to be?

2. What would individualized support look like? What challenges need to be addressed in order to implement such a system?

3. How can all teachers get on board with personal learning networks (PLNs)? Is there more that needs to be learned before this on-demand professional learning model can be truly adopted school wide?

5

Promoting Buy-In and Active Participation

So, you have formed a vision for your digital literacies initiative. You have also executed initial planning, performed a needs assessment, selected appropriate professional development models, and formulated a program schedule. What's more? You have even begun developing a digital content library. Wow! That's a lot to accomplish (and a mouthful, to say the least). At this point, you may be thinking of the famous quote from the movie, *Field of Dreams*, "If you build it, they will come." After all, the handouts are on the table, the technology is fired up, and the door is wide open. But where is everyone? (Or, why do they seem to arrive in a sort of "march to the scaffold"?)

It is time that we talk about promoting buy-in and active participation. We have touched on this a few times throughout the earlier chapters, but this issue is important enough that it warrants its own individual treatment. It doesn't happen automatically. And yes, you *should* want each and every one of your faculty members to have a positive attitude about professional development. Professional development is not the place to force-feed your faculty. There is some very compelling brain research which

> Our attitudes influence how much we actually absorb, retain, and apply from a learning experience.

suggests that our attitudes influence how much we actually absorb, retain, and apply from a learning experience.

Marketing is an aspect of professional development that is commonly overlooked or simply viewed as unnecessary. After all, teachers should *want* to improve their teaching, right? Of course they should, and most do! However, good things can be made sour when approached from the wrong angle. And what about those that are less than enthusiastic—regardless of who, what, when, and how?

This chapter presents fresh ideas for making the *positive* pitch and nurturing positive relationships in order to leverage buy-in from all stakeholders, even the FAVEs (faculty against virtually everything). It also describes innovative ways of incentivizing professional development that appeal to adults and don't require a budget.

Making the Positive Pitch

I think it is important to acknowledge the reality that no matter how exciting you make something, there will always be people who simply cannot be reached. However, that does not give us an excuse to merely count certain people out. We are faced with the challenge of leveraging the involvement of everyone.

This chapter further establishes a statement that was made in Chapter 2: Any professional development model—old or new—can work *if implemented properly*. We sometimes find ourselves spending countless hours searching for a miracle solution when the remedy has actually been within our reach the entire time. Is professional development being advertised and discussed within your school as an *opportunity* or an *expectation*? People often shy away from expectations while approaching opportunities with eager anticipation. Even though your digital literacies professional development program probably *is* required for your faculty, you don't necessarily have to focus on that particular facet.

> **Is professional development being advertised and discussed within your school as an *opportunity* or an *expectation*?**

Instead, emphasize all of the great opportunities and benefits that will be in store for faculty who participate! Work to instill an ethos of constant professional growth and collaboration among your faculty. It takes time, effort, and a careful sensitivity to the dynamic composition of your diverse faculty. In time, however, you can realize a positive difference in how members of your faculty approach professional development and how they function in general as a whole.

A school administrator once told me that one of the keys to successful change in a program or institution is to make faculty think it was their own idea. I believe there is something to be gleaned from this idea, with regard to the digital literacies initiative. Adult learners like to feel a sense of control over what they are expected to do. They want to have a sense of ownership in it. Moreover, people tend to look with dissention upon top-down initiatives. Simply involving faculty in the planning process from the very beginning can serve as an initial step to gaining faculty buy-in. Adult learning theory—or andragogy—only serves to further reinforce this idea of shared ownership.

The required nature of teacher professional development at the K-12 level tends to result in guaranteed participation and a somewhat captive audience—with a few exceptions. However, this is no excuse to neglect the affective aspects of program planning and implementation that generate positive attitudes and good feelings among participants and providers alike.

Common Challenges

A combination of research, experience, participant feedback, and many, many conversations with teachers from all walks of life has brought me to the realization that there are definitely commonalities among the challenges and issues being faced across the board with regard to leveraging teacher engagement in professional development. Chapter 2 briefly described certain technical, logistical, and affective issues that relate primarily to the quality of a session, program, or event. Here we look at issues that affect the attitudes and motivations of teacher participants. Time and scheduling are certainly at the forefront. Apathy and burnout also make the list. Finally, poor quality and a lack of substance plague professional development offerings in schools and larger organizations alike, tarnishing the image of professional development in general and rendering teachers gun shy of falling prey to yet another less-than-helpful program.

K-12 professional development providers might gain some unique insights from the opportunity to interact with a college or university faculty development unit. Indeed, at many institutions, faculty development (the generalized term that is widely used in higher education to refer to instructional improvement activities) is based totally upon *voluntary* participation. This presents providers with the challenge of actually drawing in faculty to participate in programs and events. This transcends mere affective or qualitative dynamics and becomes a matter of critical importance that is pivotal to the success or failure of a faculty development effort, whether big or small. Faculty development providers are certainly compelled to give consideration to the issues presented in this chapter.

Time and Scheduling

All teachers are pressed for time, both personally and professionally. Honestly, this tends to be true for most everyone in our busy world today. I recently saw a commercial on television for one of the large churches in a nearby city. The commercial was advertising the church's new noontime Sunday service designed specifically to get attendees in and out within 30 minutes. It boasted being aimed at accommodating today's busy lifestyle. I couldn't help but think that perhaps school leaders should approach professional development with this mind-set and aim to pack a big punch within a concise time span.

Investigate when the optimal times are for your faculty. Review the models and approaches described in Chapter 2 and include scheduling questions within your needs assessment as you plan your digital literacies program. Do teachers prefer meeting after school? If so, then how frequently, and for what length of time? What about during prep periods or during lunchtime? This suggestion will be appalling to some but perhaps appealing to others. Additional options include pre-school weeks and student release days. Experiment with online delivery—both synchronous and asynchronous—and begin to gauge how the members of your faculty receive that approach.

Pack a big punch within a concise time span.

There will be no one-size-fits-all solution; however, you can design a program that incorporates a selection of modalities that are most conducive to your faculty's learning preferences.

Incorporate time within technology training sessions for participants to actually set up the software or equipment and prepare for student use so that everything is ready to go for classroom instruction. Don't expect teachers to do this on their own time. It has been suggested that if we do not apply what we learn within 100 hours, then the likelihood of following through with it declines drastically.

Plan time monthly for teachers to get together and discuss problems and successes. Make provisions for teachers to observe their peers within the building and in other schools so that they might see new instructional strategies being implemented successfully. Pair veteran teachers with young teachers. The younger teachers are often digital natives and can usually support those who are not as tech savvy. On the flip side, this gives the more experienced teachers an opportunity to mentor their younger colleagues. But by all means, make it possible for teachers to do this within the school day and give them relief in other areas so that these provisions don't become yet another expectation that is piled on top of a schedule that is already busting at its seams. Provide additional release time through the use of substitute teachers; offer lunch as a way to encourage noontime mentoring; or when funds are available, provide a small stipend to compensate teachers for their extra work and to further validate its importance. In any case, professional development credit hours should be awarded for time spent developing curriculum. A common complaint I hear from teachers is that self-directed or individualized professional development activities are often not allowed to be counted toward required annual credit hours.

Once you are beyond the initial needs assessment, it will still be necessary from time to time to tackle scheduling issues by asking for teacher input. In these cases, web tools such as Doodle.com, WhenIsGood.net, SurveyMonkey.com, or a web form using Google Docs can be invaluable for soliciting feedback from teachers regarding scheduling.

Apathy and Burnout

Burnout often occurs when teachers become exhausted due to excessive demands coupled with a loss of a sense of reward for what they do. Teachers often cite poor-quality professional development as a catalyst for burnout, in addition to other issues such as student behavior, lack of administrative support, and a heavy paperwork load. When we think of apathy, we often look to apathetic students. However, there are many reasons why students and teachers alike develop apathy. A myriad of personal and professional issues at home and at school can feed apathy, but so can a poor learning environment. Indeed, if a learning experience is less than invigorating for the teacher, then there is no doubt it will fall short of engaging students. This applies similarly to professional development, where the teachers assume the role of the students and program leaders serve as the teachers of teachers.

Teachers need to feel good about how the school operates in order to perform the many functions of their job at the highest level. This includes professional development.

Years ago when I was finishing up my undergraduate work and preparing to be a school band director, one of my mentors told me never to pick a piece of music for my band that I did not myself enjoy. She suggested that there is no way I can expect my students to develop a love for the music if I am not first of all passionate about it. Likewise in the world of sales, you have to believe in the value of your product or services if you expect others to do the same. With that in mind, if you are ever faced with facilitating a professional development topic, activity, or program that you fall short of connecting with, then I encourage you to find someone else who can fill that leadership role with total, authentic enthusiasm.

> **Teachers need to feel good about how the school operates in order to perform their job at the highest level.**

Poor Quality and Lack of Substance

The quality of a program is most directly related to the way in which it is presented or facilitated. On the other hand, a lack of substance often means that the contents, information, or activities are somewhat empty or irrelevant.

Chapter 2 established that good professional development is job-embedded, differentiated, well-planned, cohesive, and ongoing, with a well-defined accountability system. An effective session engages participants in active learning and makes use of elements such as direct instruction, multimedia, small-group discussion, self-reflection, and extensions beyond the session and into the classroom. When sessions incorporate mostly direct instruction—or if the content is geared at a level that is too low for the participants (e.g., teaching basic iPad fundamentals when teachers are ready for advanced instructional strategies)—then a sense of apathy may begin to grow among teachers, counteracting any potential buy-in that might be otherwise realized.

One way of measuring whether a professional development program has substance is to look at what comes out of it.

When I began my first teaching job out of college, a wise, experienced colleague advised me that I should aim to *produce results* in my new position. He said that in doing so, I would make big strides toward securing the continued support of my administration while also beginning to prove myself to my new peers. I eagerly received his advice and later found myself—a rookie in the field—pondering exactly what he meant by *results*. Making that connection was definitely one of those *crucible moments* in my life as leadership expert John Maxwell (2011) would put it.

Similarly, it is important that professional development leaders provide programming that renders real results early on. Teachers need to see those results as soon as possible in order to secure their sustained buy-in and ongoing participation. Results are not always tangible in nature but may exist on an intellectual level. Teacher participants may identify results-based professional development as that which succeeds at providing them

> **One way of measuring whether a professional development program has substance is to look at what comes out of it.**

with some form of knowledge, skills, or materials that manage to meet their needs in the classroom. As simple as this may seem, it all too often does not happen. Much like a trip to the grocery store, teachers want value for their investment. While that investment may not be cash or credit, it certainly involves priceless commodities such as time, effort, and sacrificing other things that they could be doing instead.

I strongly encourage you to review the first part of Chapter 2 if you are dealing with issues of quality and substance in your in-house professional development.

Marketing Your Program

Marketing your professional development program involves various types of promotional efforts, such as advertising to teachers, generating positive publicity, and cultivating strong public relations. The goal is to ultimately *sell* your program to teachers in the form of their active participation in the program and all extensions thereof. Community relations may seem like a side step from the main purpose of professional development, but remember that community involvement is a key component of comprehensive school improvement.

An initial aspect of marketing, which occurs early on in the planning stages of a program, involves gauging the characteristics and needs of the consumer (i.e., the teachers) in order to make sure that the product (in this case, the professional development program) actually targets and meets real needs. As with any product, it is difficult to generate interest if there is no need among the target group. (Whether or not the potential customers actually *recognize* that they need something is another story altogether.)

Creating a Brand for Your Program

Part of making the positive pitch is developing that pitch. You can generate both interest and excitement by using words and phrases that are sensational, yet purposeful. Please understand that I am not suggesting that you become artificial or infuse meaningless hype. That can only hurt your efforts. Instead, consider a theme or slogan. For example, a noontime series might be called Lunch and Learn. (Be sure to specify whether participants need to brown-bag it.) I once facilitated a series of working sessions and called it a Curriculum Development *Marathon*. "What exactly was this *marathon* about?" teachers might ask. It's at that point that I had them hooked. You might offer a PD Buffet where teachers pick from a feast of options spread out before them, or open up the Tech Tools Toybox and offer new and innovative tips and tricks each time. Breakfast Bytes might provide a morning mix of professional learning, while Appy Hour could be a great way to introduce useful iPad apps for teaching and learning.

Create a logo and perhaps some other graphical elements to use. Tap your art or desktop publishing teacher or perhaps a talented student leader. Put together something sleek and impressive . . . not something that teachers will gawk at. Avoid tacky, cartoonish clipart. Do an image search online for logos and notice the clean, simple design style of professional logos. Find some logos that you like and use them as inspiration to develop your own. Again, this is definitely a point at which you want to draw upon the skills of your capable colleagues, and it is an excellent opportunity to involve your faculty members as stakeholders in the process.

Bring some creative thinkers to the table and brainstorm catchy ways of branding your digital literacies professional development initiative. Keep it real, but think outside of the box. Actually, as permission marketing expert Seth Godin (2011) says, "poke the box." It's awfully lonely outside of the box—and the inside is rather dark—so *poke the box* with your innovative marketing.

> **Keep it real, but think outside of the box.**

Advertising

Advertising efforts aim to generate interest, not just awareness. I am *aware* that the community band is playing in concert on Friday night, but I am not necessarily *interested* in attending. But wait! I just received an e-mail with the list of pieces they will be playing, and it's a patriotic theme. Later, I saw a poster at the entrance to a local restaurant with that same information. Now, I am definitely going to be there because I enjoy patriotic music. The point I am making is that I was *aware* of the event long before I became *interested* in it. Promotion increases awareness. Advertising attempts to breed interest.

With that in mind, it makes sense that plain announcements via intercom, e-mail, and mailbox can suffice as promotional efforts. On the other hand, advertising demands a compelling hook that will grab the attention and interest of your teachers. This is where that branding you have been working on comes into play.

Design 11-inch × 17-inch posters that are colorful and catchy, yet concise. Have these printed on nice, glossy paper—like a theater company would do for a show poster—and place these strategically throughout the school building. Also, set up a blog and/or website and begin sending e-mails to teachers—taking care to brand everything cohesively. You are establishing a name for your digital literacies professional development program. Use web tools such as GoAnimate, Xtranormal, and Glogster to develop creative multimedia objects. It's okay to have some fun with it. It is also entirely appropriate to leverage the power of social media to connect with your teachers. Facebook, Twitter, and LinkedIn can be used as communication channels as can any other social media platform. Create a Facebook Page and encourage your teachers to *Like* it. Establish a Twitter hashtag and setup a unique Twitter account. Teachers can follow the Twitter account and begin tweeting about digital literacies using the unique hashtag (e.g., *#DigLitPD*). Finally, set up a discussion thread in LinkedIn where teachers can network and exchange ideas. Begin to generate enthusiasm and interest well in advance of the start of the digital literacies program by pitching little contests, awards, and incentives. These don't have to be elaborate or expensive. Furthermore, this is a great way to involve teachers from the early stages of your program and give them that sense of ownership and personal investment that is so important to achieving their buy-in and active participation.

Publicity

Generate publicity at multiple levels in order to increase public awareness of the many great things you are doing at your school— namely the digital literacies professional development initiative. Emphasize the relevance of digital literacies to student preparedness and success in the 21st-century workforce. This will certainly be appealing to local businesses and industries as they look to the upcoming generation of students as potential future employees.

Publicity efforts may involve writing an article for the school district newsletter; submitting press releases to print, radio, television, and online news outlets; inviting the local education reporter to do a newspaper feature; scheduling speaking engagements at local civic organizations; and cultivating meaningful professional relationships through active participation in community events.

Invite the education reporter from your local newspaper to come and take pictures at your professional development events. If she is unavailable to come, then write an article and ask her to publish it. Oftentimes, journalists at understaffed local newspapers may not have time to write a story on request but are starving for content and eager to receive high-quality submissions.

But publicity is even more important within the school. This will almost certainly involve e-mails, flyers in teachers' mailboxes, and other forms of communication. This should not be haphazard. Develop a *Communication Plan* that includes deliberate communications, specifies the channels by which you will deliver them, and correlates with a certain day of the week for recurring communications or specific dates for one-time communications. Your communication plan can be as simple or complex as you wish. Table 5.1 provides a sample template that you may wish to adapt and expand according to your unique context.

Table 5.1   Communication Plan

Monday	*Tuesday*	*Wednesday*	*Thursday*	*Friday*
Time:	Time:	Time:	Time:	Time:
Responsible person:	Responsible person:	Responsible person:	Responsible person:	Responsible person:
Recurring action:	Recurring action:	Recurring action:	Recurring action:	Recurring action:
One-Time Communications				
Date & time:	Date & time:	Date & time:	Date & time:	Date & time:
Responsible person:	Responsible person:	Responsible person:	Responsible person:	Responsible person:
Action:	Action:	Action:	Action:	Action:

Public Relations

Cultivating public relations is certainly a part of the publicity efforts just mentioned in the previous section. Additionally, however, professional development leaders can promote strong public relations by inviting community leaders, businesses, and other partners into the school to participate as stakeholders in teacher professional development. They might sponsor certain sessions by providing snacks, door prizes, special materials, stipends, or outside trainers. During a professional development series that spans one or more days, community partners might be invited to participate in a community fair of sorts where they are explicitly given the opportunity to show their support of teachers in a special way. To be clear, the purpose of such an effort should be to encourage teachers and show community support—not merely to advertise the local businesses. Still, there will be obvious payoffs for all parties involved.

Attempting to organize a community fair during teacher professional development could easily steal the focus of school leaders' efforts away from planning and implementing the actual professional development sessions. With that in mind, it can be advantageous to delegate this to a community involvement coordinator, a parent-teacher organization, or the local community leadership council.

Finally, when applying marketing concepts to professional development, it is important to realize that the teachers actually become part of that *public* that is the target of public relations. With that in mind, relationship building at the individual level is of utmost importance. I'll further address this later in the chapter.

Making the Sale

Ultimately, all of the advertising, publicity, and relationship building in the world are in vain if you fail to hit a home run and close the sale with a well-developed and executed professional development program. While the strategies and concepts described in this chapter for promoting buy-in and participation can definitely take your digital literacies initiative from good to great, don't let it become a distraction from creating high-quality, substantive professional learning experiences.

> **Advertising, publicity, and relationship building are in vain if you fail to close the sale with a well-developed and executed professional development program.**

Figure 5.1 illustrates the flow of marketing efforts as they span throughout the digital literacies professional development initiative. Each step begins as early as possible once enough plans are in place to drive marketing decisions. They also continue into the implementation phase as you *make the sale* to your faculty through high-quality professional development activities.

The Importance of Relationships

Building and nurturing relationships is an invaluable component of developing a positive ethos among your faculty and marketing your digital literacies professional development initiative. Remember the Three Rs? Rigor . . . Relevance . . . Relationships. It seems that there are almost as many sets of three Rs in education as there are 80/20 rules in the business world. In any case, I want to urge you to consider the vital importance of focusing on relationships at the individual level as you work to leverage buy-in and active participation among your faculty.

There will, no doubt, be individuals who are slow to buy into anything new, and I am not just referring to the FAVEs. These are people who might have been around long enough to have seen a lot of *new ideas* come and go with a lot of hype and little substance. This has resulted in attitudes that are jaded toward anything that is pitched as new and better. These may also be people who are reluctant technology users.

Professional development leaders can go a long way in leveraging the buy-in of these faculty members by reaching out to them individually and working to build or strengthen their professional relationship with them. Proactively look for opportunities to visit with

Figure 5.1   Professional Development Marketing Flow

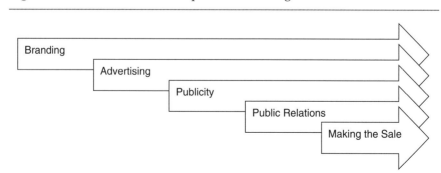

them one-on-one and build good rapport—both in general and with regard to the digital literacies initiative. Find times to catch those individuals while they are doing morning bus duty or eating lunch. Make it a point to work your way through the building on a regular basis and stick your head in every teacher's room for a quick chat during their break. You may not be able to accomplish this as often as you might like due to limited discretionary time; however, it is still very important that you get to know those teachers whom you might not otherwise see outside of the professional development sessions you led on a regular basis. They need to see that you are working alongside them and that you care about them individually—in a professional sense. This will lay a solid relational foundation when you make those personal contacts on a regular basis. Digital communications are good, too; but in this case, they are no replacement for time spent face-to-face.

Another way to build relationships and leverage buy-in is through identifying and targeting *opinion leaders*. These are the individuals among the faculty whom teachers respect and seem to follow for various reasons. Opinions leaders are definitely *not* always the same people who are in official leadership roles, so look carefully and make it a point to earn their buy-in early on. If you do this, others will follow.

Leveraging Intrinsic Motivation

In his book, *Good to Great*, Jim Collins (2001) states that given the right conditions, factors such as motivation become a non-issue. What does he mean by that? Among other things, I think he is saying that if you make ice cream that tastes good and sell it on a hot day for the right price, you don't have to worry about trying to convince the second kid in line that it's worth buying. In other words, offer a good product (i.e., professional development) at the right time and place, and teachers will be intrinsically motivated to fully engage themselves in it.

Of course, I don't want to oversimplify or even try to quantify a best practice for leveraging intrinsic motivation. You just need a bit of creativity and a willingness to acknowledge the issues that are otherwise overlooked. (I like to think of those Dyson commercials for vacuums and touch-free hand dryers where they talk about how they simply address the problems others seem to ignore.) Recognize that it is beyond your ability to single-handedly instill motivation in a room full of people. At the same time, turn your focus to addressing the issues you *can* control—all of those seemingly little things that can quickly stifle any motivation that might be growing within the teachers in your school. These things can have a direct effect on the climate of your professional development.

Breaking Down Barriers

A list of examples could potentially be endless, and each school has certain unique issues and characteristics that others might not ever fathom. So, take a moment to refer to Table 5.2 where I have provided a starting point to stimulate your thinking on this subject. I encourage you to brainstorm additional steps that you can take in order to create optimal learning conditions and promote intrinsic motivation within your unique context, which includes your physical environment, the characteristics and needs of your teachers on an individual level, and the overall ethos, morale, or climate of your faculty as a whole. Each of these areas is in constant flux, and it is your challenge to gauge them and adjust accordingly. Now, fill in the blanks with any potential issues—no matter how miniscule they seem—that might plague your teachers' attitudes toward professional development. Match those problems with solutions in the right-hand column. Use this checklist as an action plan for this component of the overall professional development initiative.

Think about the learning environment. Perhaps you can hold sessions in pleasant rooms with windows and comfortable seating as opposed to interior bunker-like rooms with plastic seating and stale air. I once moved the second day of a workshop from a plain classroom to an administrative conference room with executive chairs and

Table 5.2   Checklist: Setting the Stage for a Positive Experience

Potential Issues or Concerns	*Solutions*
❐ Meeting rooms are cave-like or unpleasant	Find a room that provides a window to the world
❐ Temperature tends to be too hot or cold	Check the thermostat well in advance
❐ Presentation visuals are difficult for some to see	Confirm the line of sight
❐ _____	_____
❐ _____	_____
❐ _____	_____

windows. The participating teachers were ecstatic! I can honestly say that their enthusiasm exceeded my expectations. And the cost of this little touch was zilch.

Be sure to check the thermostat, too. I served as a guest speaker during a daylong workshop for K-12 school leaders focused on managing student mobile devices in the classroom. It was summertime, and many of the participants were wearing sandals and flip flops. The room we met in was so cold that people were literally putting their feet inside of their laptop cases in order to break the chill. During breaks they would go outside in order to warm up. As you might expect, this frigid climate distracted the participants both mentally and physically. Not only were they experiencing a brain freeze of sorts, but they were also reluctant to pull their hands out of their pockets in order to participate in the learning activities with their mobile devices. There was not a local thermostat control—the system was managed from a central location—so there was no chance of remedying the situation once the day had begun. Since school air systems are sometimes controlled remotely, it is important to investigate this important detail well in advance of your events, especially if you are using a facility that you are not familiar with.

When using a screen of some sort to display digital content, be sure that its size and position are such that all participants can easily see the contents being shown. A good rule of thumb is to have a diagonal inch of screen size for every linear foot of distance from the screen to the furthest possible seat in the room. This means that a room that is 75 feet from front to back should have a projector screen, interactive whiteboard, flat panel monitor, or television with a display that is at least 75 inches in size diagonally.

Screen size is only half of the equation. Also remember Guy Kawasaki's 10/20/30 Rule of slideshows: Use a maximum of 10 slides, speak for no longer than 20 minutes, and set all text to at least 30-point font size. The font size should be even larger when the screen size is less than optimal according to the guidelines above (2005).

When participants cannot focus in on content being displayed by the presenter, they become frustrated, zone out, and fail to engage in the intended learning experience.

Incentivizing Teacher Participation

In addition to breaking down barriers that inhibit intrinsic motivation, professional development leaders can also take the approach of presenting incentives that serve as catalysts to leverage teacher participation.

In his book, *Educational Leadership and Planning for Technology*, Anthony Picciano (2011) presents a simple, highly adaptable professional development model. As one of the steps in that model, he establishes the need to incentivize stakeholders. This includes not only participants who are on the receiving end of training but also providers and any other key players.

The notion of providing incentives tends to leave administrators with visions of dollar signs. While it seems that nothing in life is free, I would encourage you to entertain the possibilities of how you might draw upon resources that are already in place in order to provide some fresh incentives.

> **Explore how you might draw upon existing resources in order to provide fresh incentives.**

How to Tank a Teaser

Let me begin by applauding those of you who pour yourselves into the professional development that you plan and facilitate. When you attempt to do something special for your teachers—something that is above and beyond the required nuts and bolts—you make yourself vulnerable to their often-unsolicited comments and opinions. Furthermore, you are taking a risk of whether or not your efforts will have any sort of fruitful payoff.

There is no guarantee that any incentive will necessarily make a positive impact, but I would suggest that there is great merit in the approach that you choose to take. Taking the wrong approach is what I like to call *how to tank a teaser* or *how to ruin a good thing*.

A teacher shared with me the story of an after-school faculty meeting she was involved in. The facilitator told the faculty that if they would participate in a certain tedious data analysis activity and stay 10 or 15 minutes longer than the scheduled meeting time frame, then they could have an ice-cream sandwich. Oh, and by the way, those ice-cream sandwiches are on the other end of the building in the home economics freezer, which will require a side trip for teachers before heading to the parking lot.

As I look at this situation, I see a few fatal flaws in the ice-cream approach. First of all, the teachers were asked to stay late with no advance notice. In addition, obtaining the ice cream required relatively significant extra effort that many teachers might have decided was not worthwhile, given the time of day. What might you have done differently to make this a good, rewarding professional development activity?

Another teacher told me about an end-of-year faculty luncheon where the school even provided all of the food. Teachers looked forward to this celebratory, culminating event with eager anticipation. However, when the day came, they arrived at the gathering to discover that they would be engaging in a collaborative learning activity simultaneously while eating lunch. There would be no time to visit casually as they were divided into groups and expected to accomplish certain tasks by the end of the hour. What looked to be a joyous occasion actually ended up being a working session. I do not think that the school leaders intended to deliberately mislead the faculty, but their misguided intentions tainted, if not ruined, any positive morale boost that might have come out of the community-building time.

When you are looking to provide a neat experience—whether big like a meal or small like a pencil-top eraser—be sure to consider whether it will come across to adults as a gimmick or teaser or as a legitimate reward that is worthy of their efforts. Be careful not to insult your teachers or undermine your intentions by aiming too low with your incentivizing techniques.

Door Prizes

If resources are available to offer door prizes, then consider what teachers would both enjoy and find useful. This will vary based upon your faculty, and I would once again caution you against tanking the teaser. One option is to invite the teachers to bring door prizes. Only you know how this approach would be received by your faculty. Door prizes can be a fun way to put valuable instructional materials into your teachers' hands.

Instructional Materials

Books, software, computer peripherals, and online resources are all excellent investments that can be used as incentives and embedded within professional development programs and activities. Funding may already be earmarked for professional development activities, and while those funds might not be usable for frills, they typically can be used for instructional materials. If money is not available to purchase a book for each and every teacher, then award a few books as door prizes and also make them readily available within the school's professional development library.

Another option is to rework the rollout of a new software package or technology device that is already planned for classroom installation. Give teachers who participate in certain training sessions early access to the technology and first priority for its installation. These incentives do not necessarily have to be attached to sessions that are purely based on technology, either. In fact, it would be wise to require both technical training and a session on instructional strategies for using the new software or component within the context of teaching and learning.

Release Time

Teacher leaders who are called upon to play key roles in the digital literacies professional development program should be strongly considered as candidates for perpetual release time—that is, an extra class period to focus on their professional development leadership and support responsibilities on top of their planning period that is intended for work related to their classes. In addition to the obvious purpose of providing these individuals with the time needed to plan and evaluate professional development sessions, this additional release time during the school day makes them available to provide just-in-time support to faculty as they work to integrate digital literacies into their classroom instruction.

Offer other teachers the ability to engage in peer observation, mentoring, and curriculum alignment by arranging for occasional release time where they are able to be without students for an hour or so during the school day. Establish a legitimate need and a firm plan for how release time will be used since it takes teachers away from valuable instructional time with their students. Then, make sure that teachers evaluate and reflect upon the time spent in those customized professional growth activities.

Salary Schedule Advancement

Many states have a provision in place that allows teachers to receive professional development credit for taking college courses related specifically to their teaching assignment. Courses typically would need to be related to instructional improvement or the content area in which a teacher teaches. In some places, a one-hour course translates to 15 hours of professional development credit, based upon the understanding that a one-hour course might typically meet 15 times within a semester.

At the same time, schools often include step increases on their salary schedules based upon earning graduate hours. Increments are often set at 12, 24, and 36 college hours toward a graduate degree.

Using these terms, 15 hours of professional development could potentially be connected to a 1-hour advancement on the salary schedule. If the actual salary bump does not occur until 12 graduate hours are earned, then it would require 180 hours of professional development.

With this in mind, teachers could be offered salary schedule advancements for *approved* professional development activities that are specifically related to the digital literacies professional development program. Teachers see this as money in their pocket, and it motivates them to invest extra effort into the digital literacies initiative, especially if provisions are established for counting certain self-directed activities toward earning credits.

In terms of funding this sort of incentive, school districts who work with an incremental salary schedule already have to allocate budgetary provisions for step increases when teachers earn advanced degrees, so this would draw from that same funding. And remember, it would take 180 hours of qualified activities within this specific program to actually achieve a salary increase, so there is limited potential for this to snowball.

Minigrants

There are a myriad of innovative web-based tools and resources available to enhance teaching and learning for teachers and students alike. Many of these web tools are offered on a *freemium* or free-to-fee basis. That is, they offer a limited set of features for free, while additional features are accessible only with a paid subscription to the web tool or service. This system is advantageous to teachers because it allows them to try out a web tool and use it in the classroom without having to make a financial commitment. Still, web tools that are deemed to be particularly useful by a teacher typically offer additional fee-based features that are much needed in order to make extensive use of the tool. For instance, a screen recording tool might allow users to record up to five video clips or a maximum of 15 minutes in total length under a free account, while a paid subscription allows for unlimited recordings along with editing tools that make it possible for teachers to develop high-quality instructional videos that complement classroom learning activities. The fees for these web tools tend to range from $4.99 per month to $39.99 per year, with all variations in between.

School administrators can offer minigrants to teachers who submit detailed lesson plans that incorporate specific web tools for the purpose of enhancing student learning. These minigrants can cover the cost of purchasing teachers' subscriptions to these web tools for finite periods of time. These web tools are gems that can unlock vast potential in terms of creativity in curriculum and instruction. Their low cost means that schools can make a small amount of money stretch to provide a good number of minigrants. A reasonable cap might be $50 per teacher, while most teachers would probably only be requesting half of that amount.

As part of this minigrant program, teachers not only submit lesson plans during the proposal process but also follow up at the end of the grant cycle with reflective reports and student learning artifacts showing the products and results of the innovative instruction that was made possible through the funding. A share-out session allows teachers to disseminate new ideas and strategies, while an online wiki site (perhaps a section of the digital literacies wiki) provides a venue for showcasing the ways in which the minigrant-funded curriculum projects impact student learning. This becomes a digital repository of lesson plans and instructional strategies that incorporate digital literacies, just like the professional development initiative is emphasizing.

Presenter Compensation

Capable presenters are often abused as they are called upon time and time again to lead sessions, facilitate training, and provide ongoing support to their peers. Other teachers recognize this pattern, and many become reluctant to agree to do even one presentation because they fear the invisible strings that are attached.

Still, a successful professional development program relies upon the collective leadership of teachers and administrators alike. Indeed, it is important to tap teachers for session leadership and support roles. However, it is equally important to establish a compensation system that acknowledges the time and work required to prepare for and give a presentation. Doing so will help to prevent burnout and will also generate interest among other teachers who have the potential to be skilled trainers, presenters, and facilitators.

Begin by acknowledging that it takes approximately two hours of preparation for every hour of presentation time. So, a one-hour presentation requires a three-hour base commitment, and that gives no consideration to any follow-up that might be associated with a session.

Schools can either pay an hourly wage, provide a stipend, or give release time as compensation for professional development leadership. Developing teacher leaders is an important part of implementing and sustaining a professional development initiative. Don't ruin the effort by making it an increase of their workload.

Table 5.3 summarizes the ideas and strategies described here for incentivizing teacher participation in professional development. This is by no means an exhaustive list. Take a moment to brainstorm other possibilities—whether big or small—and add them to the list below.

Making the Connection to the Classroom

As we go to great efforts to creative positive and meaningful professional learning experiences within faculty settings, we also remain mindful that the ultimate purpose is to make real improvements in classroom instruction and realize results in the form of increased student learning outcomes. This requires deliberate, concerted support as was discussed in Chapter 4.

Teachers need time to flesh out the new ideas, strategies, and technology tools that are presented in a session so that they might actually use them in the classroom. I have mentioned the 100-hour window before. It is important to apply new knowledge and skills within 100 hours of learning them; beyond that time frame, the chances of actually using what you learned drastically decline. With that in mind—and given the fact that everyone's schedule is already stretched to a breaking point—it is vital that professional development leaders provide participants with time during each session to actually apply what they just learned and make connections to their own curricula. In fact, this *immediate work time* can be a big selling

Table 5.3 Incentivizing Teacher Participation

Don't tank the teaser
Provide quality materials
Award door prizes
Provide release time
Allow for salary schedule advancement
Offer minigrants
Compensate presenters and facilitators

point when advertising a session or series of sessions. Emphasize that the sessions will not be filled with presentation after presentation and that participants will have real, dedicated work time where they can get *off the radar* of their classroom, office, or home and actually accomplish some curriculum development work. If you make this pitch and then don't follow through, then the fault lies with you. It will have a negative impact on your credibility as you attempt to further develop your professional development program. On the other hand, if you deliver on your promises, word will get around that you are doing great things and that participation in your professional development sessions is time well spent.

> ***Immediate work time* can be a major selling point for a professional development event.**

Use the strategies described in this chapter along with your own innovative ideas in order to *create a culture of participation*. The checklist in Table 5.4 summarizes the essential elements that are often overlooked when planning and implementing professional development. Use it to help you *sweat the small stuff* in your digital literacies initiative.

Table 5.4   Checklist for Promoting Buy-In and Active Participation

❐ Identify and recruit teacher leaders
❐ Solicit faculty input
❐ Adopt and implement a marketing strategy
❐ Select ideal meeting times
❐ Reserve a pleasant venue
❐ Establish an uplifting climate
❐ Offer appealing incentives
❐ Avoid using gimmicks
❐ Ensure sessions contain substance
❐ Focus on learning outcomes
❐ Emphasize practical applications
❐ Plan for follow-up
❐ Provide ongoing support

QUESTIONS FOR REFLECTION AND DISCUSSION

1. What specific challenges currently exist that seem to form barriers to gaining teachers' buy-in with regard to new or existing professional development initiatives?

2. Which teachers within the school possess skills in leadership, communications, or design creativity and would be assets in assisting with marketing efforts?

3. What incentive strategies might be feasible within the school's unique context and potentially used in conjunction with the digital literacies professional development program?

6

Long-Term Planning

Ensuring a Lasting Impact

Programs and initiatives come and go. So do people. Needs change and new ideas arise. These realities are not unique to the field of education. It happens everywhere. Nonetheless, the education system is certainly famous for jumping from one program to another, often before sufficient time has passed to see a significant impact on student performance. However, long-term planning and foresight can serve to counteract that tendency in order that digital literacies might become well embedded into the school-wide curriculum as an integral part of preparing students for lifelong success in the 21st century.

Indeed, this professional development emphasis should not be merely a 10-month focus that is replaced by something new in the following year. I need to be clear here. There is no miracle program—not digital literacies, nor anything else—that can single-handedly change the face of education. I have used the terms *program* and *initiative* interchangeably throughout

> There is no miracle program that can single-handedly change the face of education.

this book, but the most important idea that I have also stated repeatedly is that of *infusing digital literacies into the very thread of teaching and learning*. A concerted effort in the form of a program or initiative is certainly necessary to serve as a catalyst for this type of change.

But in order to achieve a permanent shift in the way we do what we do, there must eventually be a sort of automaticity that comes about, because the reality is that at some point, any *sanctioned* program must come to an end.

A phased plan for training and support that looks at year one, two, three, and beyond can provide for successful *momentum* that yields lasting results beyond what is typically seen from near-sighted professional development.

An Embedded Approach

Professional development is too often isolated on single days, which are scattered throughout the year and often adjacent to holiday breaks when teachers are naturally inclined to be thinking about time off rather than instructional improvement. This must change. Professional development needs to be ongoing with regular support and encouragement. Otherwise, it will likely fail. Digital literacies must become infused into the very thread of teaching and learning—not just something that teachers do intermittently in order to meet an expectation and check off a to-do list. It cannot be merely icing on the cake. It has to be baked into the cake itself.

This embedded approach requires fundamental changes in ways of being. Leveraging digital literacies must become *natural* to all teachers, even to the point of near automaticity. This happens over an extend period of time, much like a pianist progresses from approaching scales and arpeggios as mechanical exercises to the goal of playing them with great musical artistry within the context of classical masterworks.

Digital literacies must continue to be addressed as essential elements of instruction by administrators and teacher leaders. To move on to another emphasis and let this fall by the wayside means it will not sustain itself. Training and support should be ongoing and systemic. The share-out sessions where teachers celebrate their specific challenges and successes of teaching with digital literacies should continue. Digital literacies should remain as a documented component of daily lesson plans, and such lesson plan templates should include it prominently alongside the other mainstays like standards, objectives, and assessment methods.

By all means, do not abandon one initiative simply to go with another. No, I am not suggesting that you become stagnate or that programs and efforts should not change. Instead, I am proposing that digital literacies are not a fad that will eventually fade away. They are essentials for communication and collaboration in the increasingly digital world that is the 21st century. Therefore, situate each of the components of your digital literacies initiative so that you can sustain it on the long term. Give teachers a sense of stability and show them that they can count on this sticking around. Then, they will know that it is okay to invest themselves in it. Teachers have become less-than-

> **Digital literacies are *not* a fad that will eventually fade away.**

eager adopters after—time and time again—being asked to drop everything and jump on board a new train, only to find months later that the fruits of their labor are being discarded at the next stop in exchange for yet another new idea. Some sustained longevity is now in order, and the digital literacies initiative is the right place to invest that lasting emphasis.

Resources and Support

In order to sustain a digital literacies emphasis on the long term, ongoing support structures must be in place. This includes, among other things, the personnel leadership and technology resources that were discussed in Chapter 4. These support resources must become part of the core infrastructure of the school—nonnegotiables with perpetuity.

If one-time expenditures were used initially to fund key aspects of the digital literacies professional development program, then such funding should be added to the annual budget of the school. Teachers who were given leadership roles in supporting their colleagues in the digital literacies emphasis should be empowered to continue in their efforts. This may mean release time from students, overload stipends, curricular resources, new training, and conference travel, among other things.

Additionally, administrators must continue to openly reinforce, support, and validate these teacher leaders in order that they will be able to function effectively in their roles among faculty peers. Finally, processes and procedures that were implemented as a part of the digital literacies initiative should be instilled within the other permanent pieces of day-to-day business.

Professional Growth Plans

While professional growth plans typically change each year—and schools sometimes choose to emphasize a certain unified goal in those plans—it is essential that digital literacies be a component of each teacher's professional growth plan on an annual basis. They do not necessarily have to be the primary focus of the plan. Instead, it is actually better to push toward the point where digital literacies are tightly woven into all other aspects of instruction and professional practice in general. Therefore, when a teacher's professional growth plan closely integrates digital literacies along with other important elements of instructional improvement, the end result is likely to be better than if digital literacies stand alone.

Accountability

Another part of ongoing support involves accountability. *Accountability is an incentive that adds value to expectation.* Leaders are often reluctant to implement accountability measures because they are afraid of being held accountable themselves. However, accountability motivates the actions of those who need extrinsic impetus while validating the efforts of those who are naturally self-driven. Whatever

> **Accountability is an incentive that adds value to expectation.**

form of accountability is used, it should be consistent across the board and include systematic follow-up. Never institute a policy that cannot be enforced.

Be sure to address the following key elements when developing an accountability system:

1. Describe the purpose, goals, and/or objectives of the program, effort, or initiative.

2. Identify the resources required to accomplish the goals or meet the objectives.

3. Clearly explain the consequences or outcomes associated with any actions taken.

Certainly, there are plenty of existing performance expectations in place that provide broad accountability from different angles. Examples include the annual requirement to obtain a certain number of professional development hours, teacher contracts that include required professional development days, and of course, student assessment standards that require teachers and students alike to raise the bar year after year. But there is a

> **Accountability motivates the actions of those who need extrinsic impetus while validating the efforts of those who are naturally self-driven.**

need for a more focused accountability structure that pertains specifically to digital literacies professional development. This might exist as a piece of a larger accountability system for professional growth activities in general, or it could stand alone as an independent emphasis. The more integrated approach is likely to be most effective and sustainable.

Faculty Turnover, Base Training, and Recalibration

As faculty turnover occurs from year to year, it will quickly become necessary to provide base training for those teachers who are new to the school. Since it may not be practical to sustain an exhaustive *year-one* training regimen indefinitely, professional development planners might explore the pros and cons of starting with initial face-to-face training that is augmented with online learning modules, mentoring, and of course, professional learning communities (PLCs). In any case, the digital literacies emphasis will fizzle out as faculty leave unless their successors are quickly brought up to speed. In the hustle of everything, it can be easy to operate under the assumption that everyone knows *the way we do it* and forget that the new folks need to be brought up to speed.

On the same token, returning faculty need to be recalibrated at regular intervals in order to refine existing practices and make adjustments as technology changes and educational needs evolve. If a healthy system of PLCs is in place, then much of the recalibration can, and should, occur on a rolling basis. Additionally, and within this same structure, a train-the-trainer approach can be used to disseminate new directives and revisions in the school-wide digital literacies emphasis. In any case, recalibration is a necessary element of any effort that is to be sustained on the right path for many years to come.

Personal Learning Networks

I keep mentioning personal learning networks (PLNs) because of the vast potential they hold as channels for ongoing professional learning. Teachers can tap into the global stream of amazingly relevant knowledge and discourse that is made possible through social media

> **PLNs hold vast potential with regard to ongoing professional learning.**

platforms such as Twitter, Google+, blogs, and wikis. The importance of the PLN on long-term professional growth and the permeation of digital literacies school wide cannot be overstated. Teachers can learn *what* they want (relevance!), *when* they want (convenience!), and *how* they want (preference!). Typically the only thing holding them back is the need to know where to start. Be sure to incorporate foundational PLN training into your immediate and long-term plans. Then, validate the significance of PLN activities by recognizing them as legitimate professional development alongside the more traditional, face-to-face activities.

The Plan

As always, getting started tends to be the hardest step. A plan is essential, but it is also helpful to remember what leadership expert John Maxwell says: *Get going in* any *direction and it becomes much easier to move toward the* right *direction* [emphasis added] (2011, p. 163). So, don't get stuck in the planning phase. Move forward! How many great ideas get stuck in committee and never see the light of day?

John Maxwell also reminds us that it is better to get *something* done with excellence than to get *nothing* done to perfection (2011). I have struggled with that very concept even in writing this book. I could tweak a single chapter for weeks and never feel like I have *arrived*. But eventually I had to make the decision to set it aside and move on to another chapter if I wanted to finish the book within a reasonable time frame.

The plan we are talking about here essentially involves determining how to make the digital literacies professional development framework—described in Chapter 3 and throughout this book—become a fully integrated part of school-wide teaching and learning on the long term. While the first year's activities, by necessity, stand alone to a great extent, the efforts of subsequent years should be increasingly embedded within core practices of administrators, teachers, and students alike. Because of this, the long-term plan becomes highly customized for each school based upon its unique context. The digital literacies remain the same, but the approach to ongoing professional growth and instructional improvement with regard to those digital literacies may change.

Obviously, it is important to adopt a plan or approach that is sustainable, supportable, and reasonable. And again, don't move on to something else until digital literacies have become a part of everyday life for teachers, students, and administrators. It takes more than a single school year for that to happen. Consider planning for yearlong phases of professional growth and instructional improvement. And *don't phase out* digital literacies as an emphasis when it becomes necessary to address something else. Instead, *rebalance*.

Tracks and Strands

As new ideas, trends, programs, and elements are brought to the table from year to year, professional development has the tendency to become a hodgepodge of eclectic innovation mixed within the remnants of yesteryear. This lack of cohesiveness can make it extremely difficult to trace the relationships between each element and decipher the purpose of everything as a whole. More is not always better. In the case of professional development, specificity trumps abundance. Strive for situated, differentiated, just-in-time training and support as opposed to attempting to be all things to all people (and programs) by essentially offering too many options.

I like to compare the latter approach to one of those money tornado machines where a person steps inside a small, transparent enclosure and is challenged to collect as much cash as possible within just a few seconds while it swirls about in a flurry of wind. (Search for a clip on YouTube!) Those people who frantically try to collect the bills by reaching here and there tend to come out frustrated and less than satisfied. On the other hand, some individuals have discovered that by simply standing still and letting the money come to them, they can walk away with a much larger wad of bills. And so it is with teachers and haphazard professional development. After struggling a bit to keep up with an overload of fragmented expectations, teachers come to the realization that they can survive by simply responding with a reactive approach when—and if—any expected action is called into check.

With this in mind, professional development leaders might consider establishing *tracks* or *strands* as a way to manage multiple emphases over time and relate them to each other in meaningful ways. Figure 6.1 attempts to illustrate this concept of strands. Although at first glance they look somewhat like an inkblot test, the dots represent various professional development elements—workshops, self-documented activities, etc.—that might occur throughout the year. Regardless of the original purpose for each activity, it will relate to one or more school-wide emphasis (i.e., strand), which is indicated by the placement of each dot either within a single strand or overlapping multiples. Remove the strands, and you are left with what seem to be random dots—hence the lack of relational structure among all of your professional development activities.

Figure 6.1 Professional Growth Activities

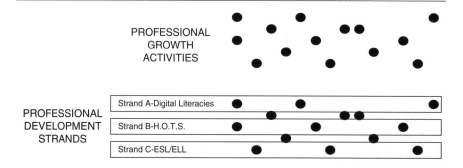

Andragogy tells us that adults prefer to know the explicit purpose when they engage in learning activities and that such learning should be situated in authentic contexts. Establishing strands can serve to meet these needs by highlighting overarching themes that really make sense to teachers and connect professional development activities to classroom instruction.

Recognition Programs

The model of using tracks or strands can be extended upon through the development of a recognition program, whereby teachers embark upon a stepwise pathway toward the goal of receiving a professional development certificate or credential of some sort that indicates they have successfully completed an instructional improvement program. Multiple certificate options are typically made available, and some degree of flexibility and choice is incorporated so that teachers can essentially select from a menu of professional development options in order to fulfill the requirements of a program.

The beauty of tracks, strands, and recognition programs is that you are primarily just reorganizing what already exists. For the most part, you are not faced with the need to develop new workshops or find money to support large-scale implementations. Think of it as reworking the menu to make the choices seem more logical—and appealing!

Recognitions or certificates can take on a broad scope or be more focused. Much like an advanced college degree, the purpose of a professional development recognition or certificate is to acknowledge specialized skills and demonstrated abilities in a specific area. A few examples are as follows:

- Digital literacies *(of course!)*
- Instructional technology (or technology integration)

- Literacy (cross-curricular)
- CCSS alignment (Common Core State Standards)
- ESL/ELL (Teaching English Language Learners)
- Online, hybrid and/or blended instruction *(could easily be separate areas)*

Teaching with technology naturally lends itself to more focused areas of certification. Such areas might include social media, game-based learning, and open educational resources (OER), just to name a few.

You probably noticed some commonalities between the sample list of strands/tracks and the suggested recognitions/certificates. Keep in mind that strands are simply topical organizers while certificates relate to a carefully prescribed set of professional development activities that a teacher must complete successfully in order to receive recognition. Of course, the act of completing an activity does not guarantee an improvement in performance. With that in mind, a recognition/certification program can be taken to the next level by focusing more on *demonstrating competencies* rather than mere participation. Raising the level of expectation will increase the credibility of the program and further emphasize the mark of professional achievement.

> **Strands** are topical organizers while **certificates** relate to a prescribed set of activities.

A well-balanced recognition/certification program includes both required elements and those that are chosen from a set of options by each participant. Table 6.1 shows a generic list of requirements that would need to be adapted to reference specific professional development activities as they relate to a particular school and its recognition/certification program.

Table 6.1   Recognition/Certificate in Digital Literacies-Infused Curriculum & Instruction

Required Activities	*Choose Two*
Monthly seminars/workshops Active involvement in PLC Peer mentoring/observation Curricular development project	Book discussion group Consultation(s) with instructional coach Online learning modules Relevant college coursework *(subject to approval)*

Developing a Digital Literacies Action Plan

So, how does all of this come together? In this chapter, I have proposed some key issues to consider when thinking about long-term planning, and I've even presented some different approaches to framing that plan. However, everything that has been discussed thus far can be wrapped up into a singular tool that is referred to as a *Digital Literacies Action Plan*. The purpose of the Digital Literacies Action Plan is to establish and articulate clear objectives and lay a detailed road map for accomplishing those objectives along every step that lies ahead. This type of plan is not one that should be developed by a single person; nor is it something that can be established in a single setting. Still, refer back to the wisdom of John Maxwell, which I referred to at the beginning of the chapter. Be deliberate, but get it done so things can start happening (2011). Approach the development of your Digital Literacies Action Plan by following this three-step process:

1. Reflect upon and articulate on paper what is happening currently in terms of digital literacies-related teaching and learning.

2. Compare that to what has been discussed throughout this book about digital literacies and professional development to support digital literacy-infused teaching and learning.

3. Set goals and develop a detailed Digital Literacies Action Plan.

As with any plan, adjustments will be necessary on a rolling basis as conditions change and various needs arise. In fact, the best way to ensure the failure of your long-term plan is *not* to monitor and adjust along the way. Your Digital Literacies Action Plan should include at least the following types of information:

- Need (*derived from need assessment; identify a problem / start with the end in mind*)
- Action step (*what must be done in order to meet the need?*)
- Rationale (*justify the action*)
- Deadlines (*in order to ensure actions are taken and progress is made*)
- Materials and resources required (*essential for budgeting and resource allocation*)
- Stakeholders/people involved and their roles (*get them involved now in planning*)
- Likely challenges (*face the facts*)

Table 6.2   Digital Literacies Action Plan

Identified Need	Action Step	Rationale	Deadlines	Materials & Resources	Stakeholders (People Involved)	Potential Challenges	Training Required (if any)	Communication Plans

- Training required (*particularly for professional development leaders/ trainers*)
- Communication plans (*how will you communicate with faculty and other stakeholders?*)

It would be difficult to adequately address all of this information in a tabular format. Nonetheless, I tend to be a global learner myself and appreciate the ability to see the big picture. With that in mind, I am suggesting that you initially develop a long-form, narrative version of your Digital Literacies Action Plan, but then also produce a more concise document with tables and other graphic organizers, which will serve as a great medium for informing your faculty at large of the plan. Table 6.2 provides a template that might serve that purpose.

QUESTIONS FOR REFLECTION AND DISCUSSION

1. What are the key resources and support structures within the school upon which the long-term success of a digital literacies professional development program may pivot?

2. How does accountability currently fit into the context of professional development? What changes need to be made in order to make it more viable on the long term?

3. Would a customized faculty recognition program be purposeful as part of the school's Digital Literacies Action Plan? If so, what might it look like?

7

The Tools
of Technology

I have spent the first six chapters of this book nearly dancing around the topic of technology tools and skills. My purpose of doing so has been to try to help readers avoid the all-too-common pitfall of getting tunnel vision and pinning technology skills as the end-all goal. Indeed, this happens much too often, resulting in students and teachers who are equipped with technical knowledge but little, if any, ability to make application and be adaptable over time.

Still, there is no doubt that technology plays a key role in digital literacies. And while technology skill acquisition is not the primary purpose of digital literacies professional development, it is a natural part of developing such digital literacies.

Wikis, blogs, and podcasts are just a few examples of technologies that enable digital publishing, collaboration, and information curation. Augmented reality applications enable users to mashup data from multiple sources into visualizations that can be interpreted in new ways that are useful beyond how such data could be used alone. Mobile devices, social networks, and multiuser virtual environments (MUVEs) are other examples of technologies that are penetrating daily life and redefining literacy in the 21st century.

Table 7.1 lists each of the five digital literacies along with their respective information and communication technologies (ICTs) and example tools that fall within each category. This chapter takes a look at these ICTs and provides strategies and resources for addressing each one within the professional development program as a whole and ultimately integrating it into classroom instruction. For each of the digital literacies, the following aspects are addressed:

- What Is It?
- Information and Communication Technologies (ICTs)
- Related Tools (i.e., Websites)
- Examples in Teaching and Learning

The descriptors throughout the chapter are written as desired outcomes or behavioral objectives that should become part of the goals of a digital literacies initiative. The purpose here is to provide technical information and resources that will assist teachers and administrators with the technological side of implementing the digital literacies in teaching and learning. Additional resources are available online at this book's companion website (http://www.digitalliteracies.net).

Table 7.1   Digital Literacies and Their Associated Information and Communication Technologies

Digital Literacies	Information & Communication Technologies (and related tools)
Locating and Filtering	Internet search, research, tagging
	*Wikipedia, Google Search, Google Scholar, Wolfram	Alpha, Zotero, Diigo*
Sharing and Collaborating	Social bookmarking, online document productivity, wikis, blogs, social networking, AR, MUVEs, identity and privacy management, Creative Commons
	Diigo, Google Drive, Google Sites, Wikispaces, Blogger, Google+, Twitter, Facebook, Edmodo, Ning, Layar, Second Life, OpenSim, Gravatar
Organizing and Curating	E-portfolios, social bookmarking, wikis, blogs, microblogging, AR
	LiveBinder, Diigo, Blogger, Twitter, Scoop.it, Paper.li
Creating and Generating	Wikis, blogs, podcasts, e-portfolios, MUVEs, Creative Commons
	Google Sites, Wikispaces, Podbean, YouTube, SchoolTube, iTunes, WeVideo, Layar, Second Life, OpenSim
Reusing and Repurposing	Virtual globes, interactive time lines, mashups, remix, fanfiction
	Google Earth, Google Maps, Dipity, Ficly

LOCATING AND FILTERING

What Is It?

The Internet is a vast and messy place. Students locate sources of information that are accurate and reliable amidst a sea of subpar content (i.e., muck!). Rather than defaulting to Google, students select from a variety of niche search engines and use strategic queries to locate specific information. They constantly evaluate information to determine accuracy, relevance, and all-around appropriateness for the given context. Teachers can help students develop this digital literacy in the early grades beginning with their first interaction with technology.

Rather than avoiding Wikipedia altogether, students understand how to use it as an information resource and make meaningful contributions to it as content authors and editors. Research databases such as Google Scholar and organizational tools such as Zotero assist with information gathering and organization at the scholarly level.

Students use social bookmarking platforms to develop tag libraries, which allow themselves and others to perform categorical searches and build upon the previous search efforts of others, rather than searching the open web every time. After all, so much more can be accomplished when we draw upon the global collective intelligence.

Information and Communication Technologies (ICTs)

Internet Search

Search engines are *not* all created equally. They use a variety of methods to index the vast Internet, and search results will vary from one to another—even with the same query. Some search engines are broad, while others focus on a specific subset, such as books, scholarly articles, images, videos, etc.

Research

Online research is a viable option, even for locating printed sources of information. While some schools have subscription-based access to research databases, there are openly available options for students who do not have access to premium resources.

Tagging

Research and social bookmarking tools enable categorical tagging, which makes it easier to locate, organize, and even share information resources.

Related Tools

Wikipedia
http://www.wikipedia.com

The world's most popular collaborative encyclopedia should not be blacklisted. Rather, students need to know how to locate information and filter content in order to identify what is useful.

Google Search
http://www.google.com

There are many powerful tools and features that too often go unused when searching with Google. Efficient online search skills are essential baseline digital literacies upon which virtually everything else is built.

Boolify
http://www.boolify.org

This kid-friendly search engine uses colorful puzzle pieces to help young users construct search queries that include Boolean operators (and, or, not), thereby rendering more strategic searches and highly targeted results.

Google Scholar
http://scholar.google.com

Scholarly articles, chapters, books, and other academic content can be located using Google Scholar, and the search engine can even be interfaced with a school's own research database in order to unlock subscription-only content while still enjoying the convenience of using Google Scholar to perform searches.

Wofram | Alpha
http://www.wolframalpha.com

This innovative search engine concept is able to interpret plain language computational queries and draw upon extensive databases to solve mathematical, scientific, logical, and otherwise complex problems (see Figure 7.1).

Zotero
http://www.zotero.org

Zotero helps students collect, organize, and share research. It is also extremely useful for creating, formatting, and maintaining a list of citations. Teachers should not be afraid to allow students to use online tools such as Zotero for citing sources. Just compare it to the use of graphing calculators in mathematics courses!

Diigo
http://www.diigo.com

Social bookmarking is a means by which students can pare down the scope of their searches and benefit from the efforts of other social bookmarking community members. The use of tagging to categorize bookmarked web pages makes organizing valuable resources extremely easy. Social bookmarks reside in online accounts that can be accessed from anywhere in the world with an Internet connection and can also be linked to mobile devices for on-the-go tagging and just-in-time research.

Examples in Teaching and Learning

• Students learn effective search skills and apply them when researching information for projects and learning activities of all scopes and types. They use specialized search engines instead of going to Google or Bing as a launching point for online information retrieval. When looking for the population of France, students use the Wolfram | Alpha computational search engine because it is known to draw from reliable knowledge bases.

• When accessing information online, students use a rubric or a self-check process to evaluate the accuracy, reliability, and validity of the information and the sources they are retrieving that information from. If learning about musical instruments, the SFSkids.com website of the San Francisco Symphony is likely to have more reputable information than a home-grown site with an obscure web address.

• Students become fluent at using online research databases (e.g., EBSCO) and develop the practice of going to those first as opposed to jumping straight to an open Internet search. The school library media specialist may be able to assist teachers in instructing students on how to use online research databases.

• Teachers establish social bookmarking groups and lists on Diigo or another service, and students contribute to those shared collections on a day-to-day basis as they are locating information for various learning

Figure 7.1   Wolfram | Alpha Search Results

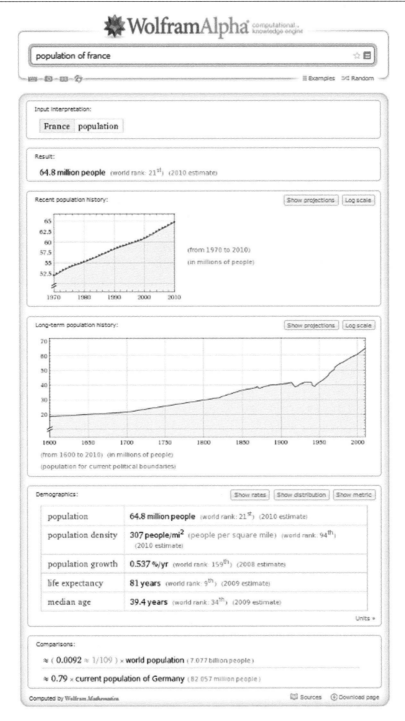

Source: WolframAlpha LLC—A Wolfram Research Company, http://www.wolframalpha
.com/input/?i=population+of+france

activities. For instance, students might collect and annotate links to excellent websites on civil rights throughout Black History Month. Students are given credit for actively participating in and contributing to this community-based online resource database. This type of compendium makes future research more efficient, enables resource sharing, and allows students not to have to start at a zero baseline every time they engage in online research.

- As part of content-area instruction, students are required to contribute to specific Wikipedia pages, adding pertinent information (and citing their sources) and editing inaccurate content. In an Arkansas history class, students might refer to local experts and notable publications in order to add or enhance entries describing the state's culture, famous events of the past, and notable figures.

SHARING AND COLLABORATING

What Is It?

No longer is the Internet a read-only venue. In sharing and collaborating, students become producers of content. They contribute to and build upon the collective intelligence, where the global knowledge base grows exponentially due to collaboration, cooperation, and competition. Browser buttons and widgets embedded on web pages make it extremely easy to share online content on the fly, without having to tediously log in to social networks and create new posts.

Students understand how their activities leave a digital trail and are careful with how they use and share their own personal information as well as that of others. They create appropriate usernames and complex passwords, and they manage them responsibly.

In a definite paradigm shift, teachers encourage students to share knowledge, information, and resources as they engage in experiential learning. Students collaborate to develop solutions to real-world problems through project-based learning and even through activities of a more traditional nature.

Information and Communication Technologies (ICTs)

Social Bookmarking

Social bookmarking allows students to share online resources via categorically tagged bookmarks. This is far more efficient than using browser-based favorites, particularly since it can be shared with others and accessed by the individual student from multiple devices.

Online Document Productivity

Web-based application software enables both synchronous and asynchronous collaboration on documents, spreadsheets, and presentations. These web apps also make it easy to share these types of projects with others for editing or read-only access. Many online document productivity apps (e.g., Google Docs) allow for importing and exporting between computer application software (e.g., Microsoft Office, etc.) and the web. Not only are these online platforms eliminating the need to attach files back and forth via e-mail, they are also enabling a new type of collaboration that ramps up the quality of writing, presentations, and projects of all kinds. Indeed, even writing—which has traditionally been somewhat of a solo act—is now a social activity in the age of digital literacies.

Wikis

Wikis enable the collaborative creation of websites and other online content using a friendly interface that bears some resemblance to the tools available in a word processing application. This ease of content authorship was not previously viable during the earlier years of web development when coding and computer-based software were the only methods by which websites could be produced. Wikis are excellent venues for project collaboration and topical information management because of how well they handle user permissions and diverse media formats. Furthermore, wikis assist with group project assessment in that they keep track of user contributions at the individual level.

Blogs

Blogs can take on a lot of different faces, but they might best be described as online journals where authors can post and readers can comment on those posts. Blogs tend to be arranged in a chronological format. They offer the ability for multiple authors to contribute, which really opens the door for broad collaboration.

Social Networking

The term *social networking* tends to be most associated with Facebook and Twitter. However, there are numerous social networking tools and platforms, and in its broadest sense, social networking could even encompass all types of social activities. Social networks can serve as venues for both formal and informal learning. Once again, the theme is collaboration, and the goal is for students to engage in purposeful interaction that transcends traditional classroom discourse and results in learning that is authentic, situated, and engaging.

Augmented Reality (AR)

Augmented reality blends computer-generated content—such as sound, video, images, text, or georeferenced data—with a real-world environment. Mobile devices equipped with AR apps and GPS are often used as viewfinders where a physical object and/or environment is enhanced by contextual information or media that essentially augments what the user sees, hears, or otherwise experiences in particular location. AR can be extremely simple or incredibly high in complexity.

Multiuser Virtual Environments (MUVEs)

Also known as virtual worlds, MUVEs are three-dimensional online game-like environments where users, represented by avatars, interact and engage in what can be highly productive activities. Massively multiplayer online role-playing games (MMORPGs) are a form of MUVE, and World of Warcraft (WoW) is one of the most well-known MMORPGs. There are some exciting implications for the use of virtual worlds in teaching and learning.

Identity and Privacy Management

The digital revolution has led to a rapid increase in the amount of personal and otherwise sensitive information that is transferred over the Internet. Students need solid guidance in the area of Internet safety across the board—from Facebook to e-mail to financial institutions. This instruction should be embedded into all aspects of digital literacies. Some people would prefer to simply avoid sharing information online altogether as a coping mechanism for issues of identity and privacy management. However, a more appropriate approach is to learn how to handle sensitive information safely and responsibly in the online environment. Indeed, in our increasingly digital world, the need to transmit personal data through the Internet is only going to increase as time goes on.

Creative Commons

As the value of openly sharing knowledge online has increased, so has the need to establish a standard by which it can be facilitated. In contrast to copyright, which limits sharing, Creative Commons provides open licenses that users can apply to their intellectual property in order to guard their ownership of that content while allowing other users to use, share, and even manipulate it according to established guidelines (see Figure 7.2). This can be a boon for students and teachers as they locate, create, and share all types of content during collaborative learning activities.

Related Tools

Diigo
http://www.diigo.com

With this social bookmarking platform, teachers can set up groups for their classes where students can create annotated lists of online bookmarks. This type of collaboration can facilitate powerful research efforts, whether the product of such research is to be created independently or as a team effort.

Google Drive
http://drive.google.com

Google Drive encompasses what has been known for some time as Google Docs. This platform features the ability for multiple users to collaborate on documents, spreadsheets, and presentations. While there are definitely alternatives to Google Drive, such as Microsoft Office Web Apps, one advantage of using the Google platform is the way in which it integrates so tightly with all of Google's other apps.

Google Sites
http://sites.google.com

Google Sites is a web content platform that functions much like a wiki, with highly collaborative functionality and user-friendly features. The way in which it is situated within Google's large portfolio of apps makes it possible to use Google Sites in concert with many different web tools to develop media-rich sites and resources.

Wikispaces
http://www.wikispaces.com

Wikispaces is a wiki platform that provides several unique conveniences for the educational environment. It enables teachers to create student user accounts in bulk by importing existing rosters. Additionally, it provides user activity tracking at a very detailed level. Other enhanced education upgrades round out the school-friendly features of this collaborative wiki platform.

Blogger
http://www.blogger.com

Like its other apps, Google's blogging platform integrates well with Google's slew of open educational resources. A single user account setup with Google enables access to Blogger as well as any of Google's other web apps.

WordPress
http://www.wordpress.com

WordPress is one of the most popular blogging platforms, and it features a vast catalog of plug-ins which infinitely expand the features and functionality of the platform. Additionally, WordPress is an open source blogging platform, which means that tech savvy educators can opt to set up their own in-house blogging platform if they wish. However, WordPress offers free blog hosting on their site, so this is an extremely viable option for users of all skill levels.

Google Plus
http://plus.google.com

Google Plus (Google+) is a social network aimed at competing with Facebook and the like. Google+ has significant potential for use in education because of its intricate privacy controls. Teachers can create Circles and place their students in those Circles so that information and resources can be shared within the Circle and collaboration can occur in a controlled environment. Google Hangouts can be launched within a Circle as a way to web conference within the class and also with outside experts in fields of study. Still, all of this can pull in collaborative documents and presentations from Google Drive for a highly integrated learning experience.

Twitter
http://www.twitter.com

Twitter is a microblogging platform where users can post short tweets of 140 characters or less, categorized by #hashtags, or keywords prepended with a pound sign prefix. Users follow other users and topics of interest in order to engage in bite-sized learning. Twitter is equally valuable as a sharing and collaboration tool as it is for locating and filtering web content. It's extremely easy to get started. And there's a lot of valuable information on Twitter. It's not just for sharing about your coffee drink. As I write this chapter, a presidential election draws near. Many of the news media outlets have tapped into the power of Twitter and measured the activity at various specific points throughout the campaign season. It is remarkable to see that several *million* tweets were sent globally during just one of the presidential debates, which lasted a mere 90 minutes. Imagine how this type of collaboration and sharing has the potential to influence the collective intelligence and make an impact on future directions. And this potential is certainly not limited to just politics.

Facebook
http://www.facebook.com

Teachers can create pages on Facebook—somewhat, but not altogether, similar to Google+ Circles—where they can post information and resources and students can collaborate to a limited degree. One of the benefits of Facebook pages is that students and parents can Like a page without gaining access to a teacher's personal profile. This also works in the opposite direction so that teachers can avoid crossing the line between personal and professional student content on Facebook.

Edmodo
http://www.edmodo.com

Edmodo is a popular social network that is intended specifically for the educational environment. It offers many useful features that are found in the mainstream social networks while also offering other learning-related features such as assignment and assessment tools, school-friendly organizational structures, and even digital badges that can be awarded based upon student performance and achievement.

Ning
http://www.ning.com

Ning actually allows users to create their own social networks. This might be useful if professional development leaders wish to establish a highly customized social network to use with the school-wide digital literacies emphasis.

Layar
http://www.layar.com

Layar is an augmented reality (AR) app for both iOS and Android mobile devices that allows users to enhance physical content or printed media with digital content. As is typical with AR, it is location based, meaning that teachers and students can develop dynamic, situated learning experiences that bring otherwise static material to life.

Second Life

http://www.secondlife.com

Second Life is a MUVE, or virtual world, that allows users to interact through avatars, which are graphical representations of a user. Oftentimes, users choose to model an avatar after their alter ego. Formerly, Second Life was used to some degree in educational settings; however, its use in teaching and learning is somewhat limited to higher education and adult learners now due to some changes in its licensing and terms of use.

OpenSim

http://www.opensimulator.org

OpenSim is one alternative to Second Life that has shown great potential, particularly due to the fact that it is open source (anyone who knows how to code can edit and make improvements) and it is compatible with Second Life content.

Gravatar

http://www.gravatar.com

Gravatar is a means by which students can manage their online identity globally by storing personal information in a single location and connecting many of their social media accounts to that profile. This is not a tool for managing financial data or other highly sensitive information; however, it can be useful for maintaining control over profile photos, e-mail addresses, and other basic personal data that are commonly requested online.

Examples in Teaching and Learning

• Students use Google Docs or another online document productivity tool in order to collaborate on chemistry lab reports, civics case studies, creative writing papers, language arts research reports, accounting spreadsheets, or health presentations. While these types of learning activities are often traditionally approached as individual tasks, teachers incorporate additional facets such as having students work together up to a certain point and then requiring them to take the collective paper and branch off in order to customize and finish it independently. This type of collaboration ramps up the quality of the end writing products and—when facilitated with a stepwise process and proper individual and group accountability— does *not* inherently lead to cheating or dumping the workload upon one person.

- Students collaborate to develop topical wiki sites that become permanent online resources for future classes and people around the world. Topics might include a novel such as *Macbeth*, turtle species, the Great Depression, or the musical works of John Williams. Each student might start by creating a separate page; or instead, each student might contribute to each page. Then, students take a second approach at collectively editing and improving all of the pages in the wiki site. Such a wiki might include text, images, videos, sound clips, and other embedded media.

- Using a blog, students write reflectively and analytically on a daily or weekly basis while reading *The Great Gatsby* or while surveying the Baroque, Classical, Romantic, Impressionist, and Contemporary Periods of music. Students can either maintain their own blogs or contribute to a class-wide blog. Teachers post thought-provoking prompts that direct students' blogging. Students are also required to respond to their classmates' posts using the comments feature that is built into a blogging platform.

- Teachers establish a page, group, or class on a school-sanctioned social networking platform (e.g., Edmodo, Facebook, Google+, etc.), and students engage in productive, informal discourse on topics surrounding the course of study. These social networks are aimed at encouraging the development of community among students and thereby improving student motivation and engagement in the class. Teachers post assignments and resources online, and students are encouraged to communicate productively. This is also an opportunity for teachers to instill within their students the ideals of appropriate online behavior.

- A social studies class establishes a #hashtag (such as #Rsvl13Pop) and uses it to microblog or tweet on Twitter about instances of pop culture as they encounter them during and after school. This enables students to collect data in context, engage in dialogue, and also organize resources collaboratively. At the end of the study, these tweets remain as a lasting collection of information and resources as well as a record of the learning process.

- Teachers enlarge the learning environment by taking students to a nearby historic site or even just exploring within the school grounds. They use smartphones and tablets loaded with augmented reality (AR) apps to access factual information about points of interest, geographic terrain, and more. They engage in situated learning experiences where a vast expanse of information is available at the touch of a fingertip. The opposite of this can also be achieved, where students actually create AR experiences for others to access. Creating AR can facilitate high-level subject-matter learning, as we know from Bloom's Taxonomy.

- Students enter into virtual worlds (MUVEs) in order to meet up with museum curators and take virtual tours of near-exact replicas of famous museums such as the Sistine Chapel. This type of immersive experience conveys vastly greater meaning than a two-dimensional web-based art gallery might accomplish.

- Much like character education or penmanship, teachers incorporate identity and privacy management skill practice into the regular flow of any given class. This is in response to the serious challenges and pitfalls students are faced with in today's digital world. Teachers work to counteract the misperception shared by many students today, which is that personal information such as log-ins, passwords, etc., are equals to the locker combinations of yesterday and that they can be shared openly to *trusted* friends.

Figure 7.2   Creative Commons Search Engine

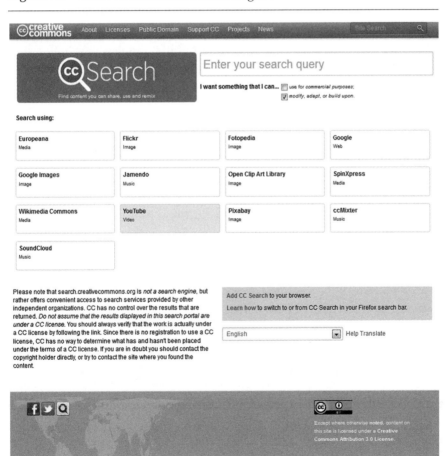

Source: Creative Commons, http://search.creativecommons.org

- Students learn how to locate, identify, and use Creative Commons content, and teachers encourage students to do so in their regular writing, projects, and other learning activities. This is in contrast to banning the use of any content that isn't created from scratch by each student.

ORGANIZING AND CURATING

What Is It?

Organizing and curating picks up where locating and filtering left off. A culture of information overload has left us struggling to keep our heads above water as we navigate the information superhighway. The only way we can stay afloat is to take an organized approach at managing the rapid influx of content that gushes in every time we search the web, check e-mail, or access a social network.

This culture of information overload and collective intelligence has resulted in a *culture of curation*. A variety of web tools are available that facilitate digital curation, where users tap into streams of information; select the most relevant, high-quality content; and develop topical collections that can be shared with others. All of this occurs on a rolling basis. Much like a museum curator is constantly improving the museum collections and putting them on display, a digital curator is using curation tools in order to strategically identify new content and organize it in a way that makes sense for personal use as well as the use of others.

While content organization might take the form of an e-portfolio, social bookmark library, or blog, curation actually adds new meaning to content by recasting it in a new context. For instance, learners might use a platform such as Scoop.it, Paper.li, or Springpad to create a curated topic on perhaps Shakespeare sonnets or healthy lifestyles where they collect all types of relevant content objects from every possible corner of cyberspace and present them in a meaningful way.

Information and Communication Technologies (ICTs)

E-Portfolios

Digital documentation is increasingly replacing three-ring binders as a method of collecting, organizing, and presenting artifacts that are indicative of performance and intellect. Web-based e-portfolio solutions offer many enhanced features such as interactivity and multimedia integration that take the portfolio concept to a whole new level.

Social Bookmarking

Social bookmarking fits within so many facets of digital literacies. Here, its purpose is as a method for organizing web links to content and resources by using topical tags, lists, and annotations.

Blogs

Journaling and reflective thinking can soar to new heights when the full functionality of a blogging platform is capitalized upon. Blogs also provide a way by which information, ideas, tools, and resources can be shared in an organized fashion. The ability for readers to comment on blog posts only enhances the collaborative aspect of learning through blogging.

Microblogging

Bite-sized information sharing can often be more meaningful and effective than lengthy narratives. Microblogging retains the chronological organization that characterizes a typical blog while keeping the post size at around 140 characters (it varies based upon the service). This format is quite conducive to mobile devices and mobile learning strategies. With regard to organizing and curating, microblogging is widely used for sharing links to articles, tools, and other social media postings, along with a brief *blurb* commentating on the linked content in order to entice readers to check it out. Learners themselves can also benefit from the rapid organizational approach of microblogging with #hashtags. (Hashtags are an unofficial method of tagging social media posts using self-created keywords prepended with a pound sign.)

Related Tools

LiveBinder
http://www.livebinder.com

LiveBinder takes the time-tested binder concept to a new level by allowing you to pull live web pages into a tab-organized workspace so that the content is always as current as the website it is coming from. There is no need to update existing content in a LiveBinder unless the source website is taken down or you decide to switch it out with something else.

Delicious
http://www.delicious.com

Delicious is another social bookmarking tool to add to the list that already includes Diigo, which was described earlier.

Blogger

http://www.blogger.com

The ability to tag and categorize posts and collaborate with multiple authors makes Google's Blogger a good option for blogging.

WordPress

http://www.wordpress.com

With so many open source plug-ins available in the WordPress developer community, there are endless possibilities for organizing and curating content and information using a WordPress blog.

Twitter

http://www.twitter.com

This groundbreaking microblogging platform is becoming increasingly prevalent in all aspects of society—to the point that educators are really compelled to incorporate it into teaching and learning. Although it originally began as a venue for *tweeting* about new shoes and great coffee, Twitter is now the host to massive *backchannel* conversations during sports events, syndicated television shows, concerts, and even political debates. This is an entirely new form of global communication that is dramatically transcending other modalities such as e-mail, traditional blogging, and even other types of social media due to its widely open format and rapid fire method of posting tweets or *microblog entries*.

Scoop.it

http://scoop.it

As a curation platform, Scoop.it makes it extremely easy to capture content and objects from the Internet and develop *e-topics* that can be followed by other users (Figure 7.3). *Scoops* can also be *rescooped* into other users' own topics. Curation is not just about sharing content though. Learners should take time to annotate their artifacts or *scoops* in order to add interpretive insight to otherwise straightforward content. Also part of curation is the act of drawing together and making connections between various pieces of information in order to make new meaning.

Paper.li

http://paper.li

This curation tool is billed as a sort of e-magazine. It interfaces extremely well with Twitter but is intended to draw from several social media platforms as well as other types of web content. Paper.li topics can be manually assembled but are typically configured to automatically generate either daily or weekly editions of this e-magazine. Learners can subscribe to a Paper.li publication, and each new edition can be set to instantly post to a social media feed such as Twitter.

Examples in Teaching and Learning

• Students create and maintain multimedia-rich e-portfolios that serve as learning logs and eventually professional portfolios to support their own advancement. At the elementary level this might include exemplary writing samples, creative math artifacts, and digital science projects, while secondary students might include original short stories, multimedia presentations, and career-based research projects. Teachers facilitate this activity and use it as a performance assessment method with the assistance of appropriate rubrics.

Figure 7.3   Scoop.it

Source: Scoop.it, http://scoop.it

- Students use a blog to collect and share resources while studying medieval art or North American climate change patterns. They discuss these resources using the blog's many features. This can also be accomplished using social bookmarking tools. One advantage of using a blog for this is the ability to also use that blog for reflection and collaborative discourse.

- Students use Twitter to tweet out links to resources and categorize them using #hashtags. They also draw upon the tweets of the global Twitter community by performing targeted searches and following experts who tweet about their topic of study. They organize these tweets and extract topic-specific content from blogs and the web in general using platforms such as Scoop.it and Paper.li. For instance, students might set up a *topic* on Scoop.it and use it to compile an annotated page that aggregates content about an upcoming holiday, a professional music group, or even the Pythagorean Theorem.

CREATING AND GENERATING

What Is It?

Everyone can be a content creator on today's Internet. Creating and generating content might take the form of web pages, media-rich wiki sites, online documents and slideshows, syndicated content such as blogs and podcasts, or virtual real estate development in a MUVE or virtual world such as Second Life or OpenSim.

As digital citizens, it is our responsibility to be contributing members of society by creating high-quality online content. An excellent example of this is Wikipedia. Too often, teachers blacklist Wikipedia due to questions of content validity and reliability. Instead, they should be teaching students how to contribute information to existing Wikipedia articles, create new articles where there are gaps in subject-area coverage, and edit those articles that have errors in order that they might be ready for other users who might not have a discriminate eye for content accuracy.

Creating and generating content should always be purposeful and deliberate, not haphazard or irresponsible. The knowledge base of tomorrow will not be limited to publisher's books and credentialed intellects of academia; it will be largely driven by the collective intelligence of content creators and generators like the students of today!

Information and Communication Technologies (ICTs)

Wikis

Because of their organizational structure, wikis are a viable option for creating and generating content, whether it is developed for students by teachers or by the students themselves as part of a collaborative learning experience. A wiki might focus entirely on a single topic of study or encompass a broader scope with subtopics organized at the page level.

Blogs

While blog posts are often of a time-sensitive nature and might not be suitable as a persistent reference, they can in fact be approached as a modular content creation platform where each blog post provides a capsule of knowledge or information that is deliberately situated within the context of the overall blog. One approach to writing an e-book is to start by blogging for an extended period of time and then begin to assemble those blog posts into a cohesive publication. Anytime new ideas, information, or resources are developed and posted to a blog, the digital literacies of creating and generating are in play.

Podcasts

The concept of podcasting stems from the mobility of the iPod and the syndicated nature of broadcast television programming. However, iPods or other mobile devices are not necessary in order to engage in podcasting. Students can use readily available applications to develop podcasts that include either audio and video or audio only. They might use the open source program, Audacity, to record audio, or they might use Windows Live Movie Maker or Apple's GarageBand to create a podcast that incorporates video with audio. Students internalize content knowledge while also learning valuable technical skills as they develop a podcast. Viewing the finished product only represents a portion of the learning experience of podcasting as a form of creating and generation.

E-Portfolios

Oftentimes new content objects must be created or generated in order to communicate specific ideas within an e-portfolio. This is different from the organization and curation that largely takes place as learners assemble e-portfolios from existing artifacts and other evidence of their past experiences and accomplishments.

Augmented Reality (AR)

While the experience of interacting with virtual objects and information in an AR environment can be stunning, even more profound is the act of developing *new* AR experiences in order to provide an enhanced learning experience for learners. As with any kind of content creation, teachers and students alike gain great insight and significant new understanding of the information being manipulated when they have the opportunity to actually create an AR learning experience. This is more than just experiencing AR as a consumer; students and teachers become producers as well—taking AR to the next level.

Multiuser Virtual Environments (MUVEs)

Although MUVEs are definitely a fascinating virtual environment for interacting with other users through avatars, many MUVEs also offer the ability for learners to actually create new content within the virtual world. This might be a museum, an interactive science lab simulation, or something else along those lines.

Related Tools

Google Sites
http://sites.google.com

As a wiki-like web content platform, Google Sites provides a place for creating and generating content to serve any purpose.

Wikispaces
http://www.wikispaces.com

Wikispaces is yet another wiki platform that can effectively serve the same purpose as Google Sites and other web development venues.

Podbean
http://www.podbean.com

This is actually a blogging platform that has been specially configured to handle podcasts and series of podcasts quite efficiently. As students produce podcasts, they might post them to a class blog on Podbean.

YouTube
http://www.youtube.com

Google continues to expand and develop the features within its video sharing site. Searching and viewing videos merely scratch the surface. Students can not only upload their own videos but also record from their webcam directly into YouTube and even edit the videos before making them available for the online community. This integrated experience has the real potential to eliminate the need for multiple tools and applications when engaging in video production inside and outside the classroom.

SchoolTube

http://www.schooltube.com

While this video sharing community does not currently offer many of the advanced features found on the back end of YouTube, it does offer perhaps a sense of security due to the controlled way in which it handles content contributors and their videos. SchoolTube has an exhaustive database of schools across the nation and requires teachers and administrators to become designated as contributors and moderators. Students can also be set up as contributors, but none of their content can become public until it is reviewed and approved by a teacher-moderator. It should be mentioned here that YouTube has now established a separate section of its site solely for educational use, and this offers great potential to leverage the enormous collection of YouTube content in a safe and controlled way where teachers, administrators, and parents all feel good about the safety of their students.

iTunesU

http://www.iTunesU.com

This version of the popular music management application is especially for education. Teachers and students can develop audiovisual learning materials such as podcasts and make them available through iTunesU. Many schools, universities, nonprofits, and other entities are engaged in concerted initiatives to develop extensive content libraries on iTunesU.

WeVideo

http://www.wevideo.com

This fully web-based, collaborative video editing tool opens the door for a high level of engagement when it comes to multimedia production as a content-area learning modality.

Layar

This AR app was described earlier and provides a means by which students can create AR learning experiences.

Second Life and Open Sim

These MUVEs have already been discussed in detail in previous sections. Both offer a venue for virtual content creation that can support extremely innovative solutions for learning needs, especially in situations where certain things could not reasonably be accomplished in real life (e.g., surgery simulations, global field trips, collaboration across vast geographic areas).

Examples in Teaching and Learning

- As content creators and responsible contributors to the collective global knowledge base, students develop wikis that contain both original and repurposed content as a way to both learn and teach others about topics they are studying in class (e.g., holidays, cultures, storybooks, polyhedrons, mitosis and meiosis, the food pyramid). Teachers provide parameters for these wiki projects and use broad rubrics to assess student learning.

- Students write blog posts as a way to synthesize concepts and ideas in a modular format that can eventually be converted into a more traditional paper if appropriate. This is also an excellent way for teachers to help students become better writers through less formal writing activities that still have structure and purpose.

- Teachers locate podcasts online and assign students to watch or listen to them as part of lessons or units on a given topic. This is also a way to facilitate a flipped classroom approach.

- Working in groups, students use simple audio and video software—even iPads or smartphones—to record and edit original podcasts or digital stories that convey original ideas and/or synthesize newly acquired knowledge about recent events, types of plants, or perhaps musical composers that have been studied in class. They then post their podcasts to a class blog or website to share with others. Students take advantage of Creative Commons content for their images, music, and other audio in order to be responsible digital citizens and pay respect to intellectual property rights.

- Teachers establish a virtual presence in a MUVE and facilitate student creation of properties, environments, and other structures in that virtual world so that students can then host others and provide learning experiences for local-to-global audiences.

REUSING AND REPURPOSING

What Is It?

Mashups and remix form the basis for reusing and repurposing. The concept of taking content and reworking it to serve a new purpose might seem a bit obscure or even outlandish. Certainly, this should only be done within the scope of intellectual property rights. However, with the strong movement toward open source data and open educational resources, the notion of mashing up or remixing content and using it for purposes greater than originally intended is garnering real attention in education and across all fields and disciplines.

In terms of digital content, this happens every day with online mapping sites such as Google Maps, while elsewhere, literature enthusiasts are remixing plots, characters, and story lines and rendering compelling fanfiction novels. Web content is becoming increasingly modular so that it can be manipulated and used across many different platforms and interfaces. Cultural remix is inundating the social web and the television programming we watch at night.

Much like arranging music can serve as a starting point for an aspiring composer, reusing and repurposing is a means by which to develop literacy skills within the context of teaching and learning.

Information and Communication Technologies (ICTs)

Virtual Globes

Virtual globes mashup content from multiple sources in order to allow users to make geographical connections at all ranges of complexity. Google Earth and Google Maps are likely the first to come to your mind, although there are many other virtual globes online that serve numerous purposes from niche ideas to highly specialized professional applications.

Interactive Time Lines

Whereas virtual globes mashup content in a geographic context, interactive time lines use the mashup concept in order to bring dates and chronology to life through embedded multimedia objects.

Fanfiction

Fanfiction is a form of literary remix where enthusiasts use characters, plot components, and other key elements from works of literature in order to create what might otherwise be called *spinoffs* of the original work. Remix has actually been happening for many years and in many disciplines—think Star Wars, and more recently, Lord of the Rings and The Twilight Saga. Increasingly, pop music seems to pay tribute to both the legends and even the hits of the not-so-distant past. And even those of us who don't have a refined eye for art can surely recognize the existence of remix in the visual arts.

Related Tools

Google Earth
http://earth.google.com

This virtual globe application is highly interactive and pulls map data from many different mapping services in both the public and private sectors. One of the many valuable features for learning is the ability for users to pin their own georeferenced content within Google Earth. These content objects might be photos taken at a specific location or even videos that have been uploaded to YouTube. Websites such as Google Lit Trips have developed very impressive learning experiences that integrate Google Earth as a mashup within the context of the study of major literary works. Explore that website and then consider how you might use mashups (Google Earth or any others) to greatly enhance your students' learning experiences without ever stepping aside from the focused study of your content area.

Google Maps
http://maps.google.com

Google Maps is web based, and while it shares some of the same features that Google Earth offers, it also has its own unique facets. Just one of them is the ability to connect with your Google account and integrate maps with other apps.

Dipity
http://www.dipity.com

This is just one of many interactive time line tools that can be found online and exploited for the purposes of teaching and learning (Figure 7.4).

Ficly

http://www.ficly.com

This fanfiction site actually fosters the collaborative generation and sharing of fanfiction works by serving as a specialized social network where fanfiction enthusiasts can hang out and write.

Examples in Teaching and Learning

• Students access virtual globes such as Google Earth in order to make connections between geographic locations referenced in literature, history, music, art, etc., and actual places on Earth as they appear in the present day. These interactive learning experiences are often further augmented by photos and videos that have been uploaded and attached to the virtual globe by other users worldwide. Students can also attach their own multimedia objects if appropriate.

• Students develop interactive time lines in order to better understand chronological relationships in history, music, literature, or any other subject. These can then be linked or embedded on a class website, blog, wiki, social networking site, or other web presence. Students can also add this type of multimedia object to an e-portfolio.

• To promote creativity and generate a deeper understanding of the subject matter, teachers challenge students to develop high-quality fanfiction. Literacy teachers might have students write *spinoff* stories, while art students could create original artwork with deliberate inspirations from a popular work. Students are expected to make concrete connections between the influential work and their original creation. This might take the form of a written reflection, a blog entry, a podcast, or a presentation.

Figure 7.4 Interactive Time Line Created on Dipity.com

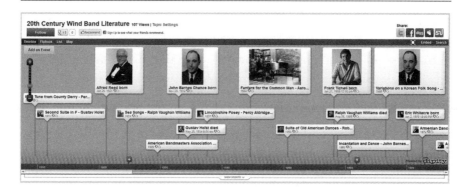

Source: http://www.dipity.com/emusictech/ (created by Dustin Summey)

Mobile Learning

The movement toward mobile devices in teaching and learning is stronger than ever. Mobile technology has a definite place within the context of digital literacies because it serves as a primary tool for both managing information and facilitating communication in our highly digital world that is the 21st century. Like everything else in the digital literacies, teachers are *not* being charged with the task of *teaching* students how to use their devices. Instead, teachers are called upon to devise and integrate instructional strategies that make creative and meaningful use of mobile technologies in order to make learning relevant for students and prepare them for a future that will rely increasingly on mobile devices.

We often operate under the assumption that students already know how to use their mobile devices and do not need additional instruction. This is only partly true. Indeed, students who have mobile devices are very likely to know how to use it in a technological sense. In fact, their abilities probably expand to the social realm as well. However, where students too often fall short is in using mobile devices for academic and professional productivity within the context of school-based learning and beyond that into the working world. This is where the digital literacies come into play. It is why mobile learning must be embraced and capitalized upon for the advantage of teachers and students alike. Consider the direction the world is going with regard to mobile technology; then acknowledge the fact that we must prepare students for what the future may hold in that respect. It's truly exciting!

Digital Literacies Integration Plan

Chapter 6 discussed the need for a long-term administrative plan at the broader program level. However, detailed planning is also essential on the part of each teacher in order that he or she might realize actual results in teaching and learning with the digital literacies.

A digital literacies instructional integration plan is one way this type of plan can be established. A sample template is included as Figure 7.5. This plan serves as an invaluable tool for articulating exactly what will happen in the classroom. It can even be incorporated into a teacher's overall professional growth plan. Here are some questions to consider when developing a digital literacies instructional integration plan:

1. What are some specific instructional needs or student learning outcomes that might potentially be met in part or in whole through the tools and competencies that comprise digital literacies?

2. How might the digital literacies play a key role in addressing the Common Core State Standards and/or other content area standards?

3. Do digital literacies provide a *relative advantage* over other *non-digital* instructional methods? (Sometimes this is not immediately evident.)

4. Which of the digital literacies are relevant to the knowledge and skills being taught within the context of each instructional strategy?

5. What information and communication technologies (i.e., technology tools) might be useful in facilitating this teaching and learning experience? Do students have access to those technologies within the school day and/or outside of school hours?

These are just a few of the questions you should consider when formulating an individualized plan for integrating digital literacies into your curriculum and instruction. The Internet will serve as a rich source of ideas and resources as you ponder new ways of teaching that leverage the digital literacies in order to equip students with the skills they need in order to manage information and communication in the 21st century.

While I do not want you to shy away from trying new things merely because you cannot envision how it will turn out in the end, I do want to encourage you to always consider the *relative advantage* factor. Relative advantage refers to the evaluation of whether or not new instructional approaches are likely to result in a higher level of student learning compared to previously used methods. This will help you avoid implementing change for the sake of change and discourage you from assuming that teaching with technology provides an advantage in itself over low-tech or no-tech alternatives. As strong of a proponent as I am of instructional technology, I never adopt or use a digital tool or strategy unless it clearly serves a purposeful role in improving student learning.

This book's companion website (http://www.digitalliteracies.net) contains resources to further supplement this chapter's treatment of information and communication technologies within the context of the digital literacies. The site provides a collaborative venue to support

Figure 7.5 Digital Literacies Instructional Integration Plan

Course(s): _____   Instructor: _____

Locating and Filtering	Creating and Generating	Sharing and Collaborating	Organizing and Curating	Reusing and Repurposing	Technology Tools (ICT's)	Instructional Strategies	Expected Outcomes	Relative Advantage

discourse among educators with regard to digital literacies. Also included are up-to-date links to tutorials, curriculum examples, and other resources that change too often to be printed on the page of a book.

It is my hope that you will choose to engage as an active contributor within the online community of educators who are all embarking upon a journey of transforming teaching and learning through digital literacies and preparing students for success in the increasingly digital world that is the 21st century. As we leverage the exponential benefits of our collective intelligence, we can realize results far greater than what can ever be attained if we go at it alone. I'll see you online.

References

Collins, J. (2001). *Good to great*. New York, NY: HarperCollins.

Godin, S. (2011). *Linchpin*. New York, NY: Portfolio.

Kawasaki, G. (2005, December 30). The 10/20/30 rule of PowerPoint. Retrieved from http://blog.guykawasaki.com/2005/12/the_102030_rule.html

Maxwell, J. (2011). *The 5 levels of leadership*. New York, NY: Center Street.

Picciano, A. (2011). *Educational leadership and planning for technology* (5th ed.). Upper Saddle River, NJ: Pearson.

Prensky, M. (2005, December 2). Shaping tech for the classroom [Web log post]. Edutopia. Retrieved from http://www.edutopia.org/adopt-and-adapt-shaping-tech-for-classroom

Summey, D. (2013). Mobile learning strategies for K–12 professional development. In Z. Berge & L. Muilenburg, *Handbook of mobile learning*. New York, NY: Routledge.

Index